THE
CRISIS
AHEAD

Ellen White
Comments on

THE CRISIS AHEAD

Robert W. Olson, compiler

REVIEW AND HERALD® PUBLISHING ASSOCIATION
HAGERSTOWN, MD 21740

This book was
Edited by Jeannette R. Johnson
Copyedited by James Cavil
Designed by Bill Kirstein
Electronic makeup by Shirley M. Bolivar
Cover graphic by Photodisc
Typeset: 11/13 Usherwood Book

PRINTED IN U.S.A.

04 03 02 01 00   5 4 3 2 1

R&H Cataloging Service

White, Ellen Gould (Harmon), 1827-1915.
    Ellen White comments on the crisis ahead: answers to questions
about the end-time. Compiled by Robert W. Olson.

    1. Eschatology.   2. End of the world.   3. Second Coming.
I. Olson, Robert W., comp.   II. Title.

236.9

ISBN 0-8280-1525-2

CONTENTS

INTRODUCTION

This compilation was originally prepared for use in the Gift of Prophecy class at Pacific Union College. It is not an attempt to finalize dogmatically on the sequence of future events, but rather a gathering together, for study purposes, of the most important E. G. White statements relating to those prophecies that remain to be fulfilled prior to the return of Christ. These quotations have been outlined in what appears to me to be a logical order, but this has been done without prejudice toward alternate or opposite views held by others.

It is impossible to arrange the chapters in perfect sequence since so many of them include overlapping material. For example, the "Latter Rain" and the "Loud Cry" are parallel experiences, one the cause and the other the effect. "Satan's Personation of Christ" might have been located near "The Close of Probation," but it seems best to study this topic in connection with "Satan's Miracles."

The Lord instructed Sister White to "charge the teachers in our schools to prepare the students for what is coming upon the world" (FE 526, 527). And the Lord gave that same prophet the information that is reproduced in this syllabus. May its study be rewarding to each student.

—Robert W. Olson

KEY TO ABBREVIATIONS

THE CRISIS AHEAD

What indications are there in the Scripture that a terrible time of trouble lies ahead of us? Dan. 12:1.

For the wicked: Rev. 14:9, 10; Rev. 16.

For the righteous: Rev. 13:15-17.

How does Mrs. White describe the period of distress that is coming on our world?

A terrible crisis. "The work which the church has failed to do in a time of peace and prosperity she will have to do in a terrible crisis, under most discouraging, forbidding circumstances" (5T 463 [Ev 31]).

The last great crisis. "In this time of prevailing iniquity we may know that the last great crisis is at hand. When the defiance of God's law is almost universal, when His people are oppressed and afflicted by their fellow men, the Lord will interpose" (COL 178).

"The calamities by land and sea, the unsettled state of society, the alarms of war, are portentous. They forecast approaching events of the greatest magnitude.

"The agencies of evil are combining their forces and consolidating. They are strengthening for the last great crisis. Great changes are soon to take place in our world, and the final movements will be rapid ones" (9T 11).

The most momentous struggle of the ages. "A great crisis awaits the people of God. A crisis awaits the world. The most momentous struggle of all the ages is just before us" (5T 711).

The crisis of the ages. "We are standing on the threshold of the crisis of the ages. In quick succession the judgments of God will follow one another—fire, and flood, and earthquake, with war and bloodshed. We are not to be surprised at this time by events both great and decisive; for the angel of mercy cannot remain much longer to shelter the impenitent" (PK 278).

The greatest crisis since time began. "We are coming to a crisis which, more than any previous time since the world began, will demand the entire consecration of every one who has named the name of Christ" (GW 323).

A stupendous crisis. "The present is a time of overwhelming interest to all living. Rulers and statesmen, men who occupy positions of trust and authority, thinking men and women of all classes, have their attention fixed upon the events taking place about us. They are watching the relations that exist among the nations. They observe the intensity that is taking possession of every earthly element, and they recognize that something great and decisive is about to take place—that the world is on the verge of a stupendous crisis" (PK 537 [Ev 703, 704; Ed 179]).

A storm. "A storm is arising that will wrench and test the spiritual foundation of every one to the utmost" (5T 129).

"A storm is coming, relentless in its fury. Are we prepared to meet it?" (8T 315).

"The storm is coming, the storm that will try every man's faith, of what sort it is. Believers must now be firmly rooted in Christ, or else they will be led astray by some phase of error. Let your faith be substantiated by the Word of God. Grasp firmly the living testimony of truth. Have faith in Christ as a personal Saviour. He has been and ever will be our Rock of Ages" (Ev 361, 362).

A tempest. "God has revealed what is to take place in the last days, that His people may be prepared to stand against the tempest of opposition and wrath" (5T 452).

"The tempest is coming, and we must get ready for its fury by having repentance toward God and faith toward our Lord Jesus Christ. The Lord will arise to shake terribly the earth. We shall see troubles on all sides. Thousands of ships will be hurled into the depths of the sea. Navies will go down, and human lives will be sacrificed by millions. Fires will break out unexpectedly, and no human effort will be able to quench them. The palaces of earth will be swept away in the fury of the flames. Disasters by rail will become more and more frequent; confusion, collision, and death without a moment's warning will occur on the great lines of travel. The end is near, probation is closing. Oh, let us seek God while He may be found, call upon Him while He is near!" (MYP 89, 90).

The most terrible conflict ever witnessed. "The conflict that is right upon us will be the most terrible ever witnessed" (6T 407).

A fearful conflict. "Satan is marshaling his hosts; and are we individually prepared for the fearful conflict that is just before us? Are we preparing our children for the great crisis?" (AH 186).

The grand test. "If the believers in the truth are not sustained by their faith in these comparatively peaceful days, what will uphold them when the grand test comes and the decree goes forth against all those who will not worship the image of the beast and receive his mark in their foreheads or in their hands? This solemn period is not far off. Instead of becoming weak and irresolute, the people of God should be gathering strength and courage for the time of trouble" (4T 251).

A great terror. "Transgression has almost reached its limit. Confusion fills the world, and a great terror is soon to come upon human beings. The end is very near" (8T 28).

Are the inhabitants of heaven aware of our coming conflict?

"The whole universe is looking with inexpressible interest to see the closing work of the great controversy between Christ and Satan" (5T 526).

Are most of the inhabitants of the earth equally aware of impending events?

"We who know the truth should be preparing for what is soon to break upon the world as an overwhelming surprise" (8T 28).

"Christians should be preparing for what is soon to break upon the world as an overwhelming surprise, and this preparation they should make by diligently studying the Word of God and striving to conform their lives to its precepts. . . . God calls for a revival and a reformation" (PK 626).

Do we as Seventh-day Adventists have a true appreciation of the crisis ahead?

"The 'time of trouble, such as never was,' is soon to open upon us; and we shall need an experience which we do not now possess and which many are too indolent to obtain. It is often the case that trouble is greater in anticipation than in reality; but this is not true of the crisis before us. The most vivid presentation cannot reach the magnitude of the ordeal" (GC 622).

"We are on the very verge of the time of trouble, and perplexities that are scarcely dreamed of are before us" (9T 43).

Is it possible for Christians to be unprepared for coming trouble, in spite of previous warnings?

Mark 8:31, 32; 9:31; 10:32-34; Matt. 26:56; Luke 24:6-8.

Why were the disciples so totally unprepared?

"They could not tolerate the thought that He in whom all their hopes centered should suffer an ignominious death. The words which they needed to remember were banished from their minds; and when the time of trial came, it found them unprepared. The death of Jesus as fully destroyed their hopes as if He had not forewarned them" (GC 594).

"Peter did not desire to see the cross in the work of Christ" (DA 415).

Has the Lord given us a clear outline of events connected with the close of probation?

"The events connected with the close of probation and the work of preparation for the time of trouble are clearly presented. But multitudes have no more understanding of these important truths than if they had never been revealed" (GC 594).

"He has a chart pointing out every waymark on the heavenward journey, and he ought not to guess at anything" (*ibid.* 598).

"We are to see in history the fulfillment of prophecy, to study the workings of Providence in the great reformatory movements, and to understand the progress of events in the marshaling of the nations for the final conflict of the great controversy" (MH 441, 442 [8T 307]).

Does this mean that we can understand every single detail of anticipated events before they come to pass?

"The mark of the beast is exactly what it has been proclaimed to be. Not all in regard to this matter is yet understood, nor will it be understood until the unrolling of the scroll" (6T 17; 8T 159).

"Much upon these things has been shown to me, but I

can only present a few ideas to you. Go to God for your-selves, pray for divine enlightenment, that you may know that you do know what is truth, that when the wonderful miracle-working power of Satan shall be displayed, and the enemy shall come as an angel of light, you may distinguish between the genuine work of God and the imitative work of the powers of darkness" (RH Dec. 24, 1889).

How important is it for us to study the prophecies that relate to the last days?

"As we near the close of this world's history, the prophecies relating to the last days especially demand our study" (COL 133).

"They should know the things that will come to pass before the closing up of the world's history. These things concern our eternal welfare, and teachers and students should give more attention to them" (6T 129).

"I then saw the third angel. Said my accompanying angel, 'Fearful is his work. Awful is his mission. He is the angel that is to select the wheat from the tares, and seal, or bind, the wheat for the heavenly garner. These things should engross the whole mind, the whole attention'" (EW 118).

"In the night season these words were spoken to me: 'Charge the teachers in our schools to prepare the students for what is coming upon the world'" (FE 526, 527).

"But there is a day that God hath appointed for the close of this world's history: 'This gospel of the kingdom shall be preached in all the world for a witness unto all na-tions; and *then* shall the end come.' Prophecy is fast ful-filling. More, much more, should be said about these tremendously important subjects" (*ibid.* 335).

"Let the watchmen now lift up their voice and give the message which is present truth for this time. Let us show the people where we are in prophetic history" (5T 716).

"Great pains should be taken to keep this subject before the people. The solemn fact is to be kept not only before the people of the world, but before our own churches also, that the day of the Lord will come suddenly, unexpectedly. The fearful warning of the prophecy is addressed to every soul. Let no one feel that he is secure from the danger of being surprised. Let no one's interpretation of prophecy rob you of the conviction of the knowledge of events which show that this great event is near at hand" (FE 336).

What are we specifically warned not to do?

"There is a time of trouble coming to the people of God, but we are not to keep that constantly before the people, and rein them up to have a time of trouble beforehand. There is to be a shaking among God's people, but this is not the present truth to carry to the churches" (1SM 180 [2SM 13]).

"There are stormy times before us, but let us not utter one word of unbelief or discouragement" (ChS 136).

In view of the approaching crisis, what should we now be doing?

"If God has ever spoken by me, the time will come when you will be brought before councils, and every position of truth which you hold will be severely criticized. The time that so many are now allowing to go to waste should be devoted to the charge that God has given us of preparing for the approaching crisis" (5T 717).

Who only will stand through the last great conflict?

"None but those who have fortified the mind with the truths of the Bible will stand through the last great conflict" (GC 593).

"Study your Bible as you have never studied it before.

Unless you arise to a higher, holier state in your religious life, you will not be ready for the appearing of our Lord" (5T 717).

"Only those who have been diligent students of the Scriptures and who have received the love of the truth will be shielded from the powerful delusion that takes the world captive" (GC 625).

THE UNION
OF THE CHURCHES

Will every Protestant denomination in America enter into the coming union of the churches?

"When the leading churches of the United States, uniting upon such points of doctrine as are held by them in common, shall influence the state to enforce their decrees and to sustain their institutions, then Protestant America will have formed an image of the Roman hierarchy, and the infliction of civil penalties upon dissenters will inevitably result" (GC 445).

Upon what basis will the Protestant churches eventually unite?

"The wide diversity of belief in the Protestant churches is regarded by many as decisive proof that no effort to secure a forced uniformity can ever be made. But there has been for years, in churches of the Protestant faith, a strong and growing sentiment in favor of a union based upon common points of doctrine. To secure such a union, the discussion of subjects upon which all were not agreed— however important they might be from a Bible standpoint—must necessarily be waived" (*ibid.* 444).

What are the two principal erroneous doctrines held in common by the churches?

"Through the two great errors, the immortality of the soul and Sunday sacredness, Satan will bring the people under his deceptions. While the former lays the foundation of spiritualism, the latter creates a bond of sympathy with Rome" (*ibid.* 588).

Will Protestantism eventually reunite with Catholicism?

"The Word of God teaches that these scenes [suppression of the Sabbath] are to be repeated as Roman Catholics and Protestants shall unite for the exaltation of the Sunday" (*ibid.* 578).

"How the Roman church can clear herself from the charge of idolatry we cannot see. . . . And this is the religion which Protestants are beginning to look upon with so much favor, and which will eventually be united with Protestantism" (RH June 1, 1886).

Will there be organizational unity or unity of action?

"Romanism in the Old World and apostate Protestantism in the New will pursue a similar course toward those who honor all the divine precepts" (GC 616).

Will Rome change or will Protestantism change in order to make this reunion possible?

"This union will not, however, be effected by a change in Catholicism; for Rome never changes. She claims infallibility. It is Protestantism that will change. The adoption of liberal ideas on its part will bring it where it can clasp the hand of Catholicism. 'The Bible, the Bible, is the foundation of our faith' was the cry of Protestants in Luther's time, while the Catholics cried, 'The Fathers, custom, tradition.' Now many Protestants find it difficult to prove their doctrines from the Bible, and yet they have not the moral courage to accept the truth which involves a cross; therefore they are fast coming to the ground of Catholics. . . . Yes, the Protestants of the nineteenth century are fast approaching the Catholics in their infidelity concerning the Scriptures" (RH June 1, 1886).

"When Protestantism shall stretch her hand across the gulf to grasp the hand of the Roman power, when she shall reach over the abyss to clasp hands with spiritualism, when, under the influence of this threefold union, our country shall repudiate every principle of its Constitution as a Protestant and republican government, and shall make provision for the propagation of papal falsehoods and delusions, then we may know that the time has come for the marvelous working of Satan and that the end is near" (5T 451).

"Protestantism shall give the hand of fellowship to the Roman power. Then there will be a law against the Sabbath of God's creation, and then it is that God will do His 'strange work' in the earth" (7BC 910).

How powerful will the Papacy eventually become here in America?

"[Protestants] are opening the door for the papacy to regain in Protestant America the supremacy which she has lost in the Old World" (GC 573).

Who will lead the people as they unite to oppose the followers of God?

"As we approach the last crisis, it is of vital moment that harmony and unity exist among the Lord's instrumentalities. The world is filled with storm and war and variance. Yet under one head—the papal power—the people will unite to oppose God in the person of His witnesses. This union is cemented by the great apostate" (7T 182).

In reality who stands behind the pope?

"There is one pointed out in prophecy as the man of

sin. He is the representative of Satan. . . . Here is Satan's right-hand man ready to carry on the work that Satan commenced in heaven, that of trying to amend the law of God. And the Christian world has sanctioned his efforts by adopting this child of the Papacy—the Sunday institution" (7BC 910; RH Mar. 9, 1886).

What should we be doing now, in order to meet Christendom's combined opposition successfully?

"The world is against us, the popular churches are against us, the laws of the land will soon be against us. If there was ever a time when the people of God should press together, it is now" (5T 236).

The National Sunday Law

What does the Bible say about the homage that Protestant America will pay to the Roman Catholic power?
Rev. 13:11-17.

When will this prophecy be fulfilled?

"The prophecy of Revelation 13 declares that the power represented by the beast with lamblike horns shall cause 'the earth and them which dwell therein' to worship the papacy—there symbolized by the beast 'like unto a leopard.' . . . This prophecy will be fulfilled when the United States shall enforce Sunday observance, which Rome claims as the special acknowledgment of her supremacy" (GC 578, 579).

"The enforcement of Sundaykeeping on the part of Protestant churches is an enforcement of the worship of the papacy" (*ibid.* 448, 449).

Where will the pressure for Sunday legislation come from?

"The dignitaries of church and state will unite to bribe, persuade, or compel all classes to honor the Sunday. The lack of divine authority will be supplied by oppressive enactments. Political corruption is destroying love of justice and regard for truth; and even in free America, rulers and legislators, in order to secure public favor, will yield to the popular demand for a law enforcing Sunday observance" (*ibid.* 592 [see also 4SP 410]).

"To secure popularity and patronage, legislators will yield to the demand for a Sunday law" (5T 451).

"Legislators will yield to the demand for Sunday laws" (PK 606).

"The Protestants of the United States will be foremost in stretching their hands across the gulf to grasp the hand of spiritualism; they will reach over the abyss to clasp hands with the Roman power; and under the influence of this threefold union, this country will follow in the steps of Rome in trampling on the rights of conscience" (GC 588).

"If the people can be led to favor a Sunday law, then the clergy intend to exert their united influence to obtain a religious amendment to the Constitution, and compel the nation to keep Sunday" (RH Extra Dec. 24,1889).

Do these Sunday-law advocates realize what they are doing?

"There are many, even of those engaged in this movement for Sunday enforcement, who are blinded to the results which will follow this action. They do not see that they are striking directly against religious liberty. There are many who have never understood the claims of the Bible Sabbath and the false foundation upon which the Sunday institution rests" (5T 711).

"They are working in blindness. They do not see that if a Protestant government sacrifices the principles that have made them a free, independent nation, and through legislation brings into the Constitution principles that will propagate papal falsehood and papal delusion, they are plunging into the Roman horrors of the Dark Ages" (RH Extra Dec. 11, 1888).

"There is a satanic force propelling the Sunday movement, but it is concealed. Even the men who are engaged in the work, are themselves blinded to the results which will follow their movement" (RH Jan. 1, 1889; 7BC 975).

Who actually is the chief mastermind of Sunday legislation?

"Not a move has been made in exalting the idol sabbath, in bringing around Sunday observance through legislation, but Satan has been behind it, and has been the chief worker" (7BC 977).

"When the legislature frames laws which exalt the first day of the week, and put it in the place of the seventh day, the device of Satan will be perfected" (*ibid.* 976).

Upon whom does a Sunday law cast contempt?

"A more decided effort will be made to exalt the false sabbath, and to cast contempt upon God Himself by supplanting the day He has blessed and sanctified" (*ibid.*).

Are we to expect Sunday laws in certain states only, or will the United States Congress take legislative action?

"Our land is in jeopardy. The time is drawing on when its legislators shall so abjure the principles of Protestantism as to give countenance to Romish apostasy. The people for whom God has so marvelously wrought, strengthening them to throw off the galling yoke of popery, will by a national act give vigor to the corrupt faith of Rome, and thus arouse the tyranny which only waits for a touch to start again into cruelty and despotism" (4SP 410 [1884]; ST July 4, 1899).

"We see that efforts are being made to restrict our religious liberties. The Sunday question is now assuming large proportions. An amendment to our Constitution is being urged in Congress, and when it is obtained, oppression must follow" (RH Dec. 18, 1888 [see also 5T 711]).

"There is soon to open before us a period of overwhelming interest to all living. The controversies of the past are to be revived; new controversies will arise. The scenes to be enacted in our world are not yet even dreamed of. Satan is at work through human agencies. Those who are making an effort to change the Constitution and secure a law enforcing Sunday observance little realize what will be the result. A crisis is just upon us" (5T 753).

"When our nation shall so abjure the principles of its government as to enact a Sunday law, Protestantism will in this act join hands with popery" (*ibid.* 712).

"A great crisis awaits the people of God. Very soon our nation will attempt to enforce upon all the observance of the first day of the week as a sacred day. In doing this, they will not scruple to compel men against the voice of their own conscience to observe the day the nation declares to be the Sabbath" (RH Extra Dec. 11, 1888).

"When the law of God has been made void, and apostasy becomes a national sin, the Lord will work in behalf of His people" (*ibid.* Dec. 24, 1889).

"By the decree enforcing the institution of the papacy in violation of the law of God, our nation will disconnect herself fully from righteousness" (5T 451).

Will the United States continue to be a favored nation after it has legally set aside the law of God?

"The people of the United States have been a favored people; but when they restrict religious liberty, surrender Protestantism, and give countenance to popery, the measure of their guilt will be full, and 'national apostasy' will be registered in the books of heaven" (RH May 2, 1893).

"So may this apostasy be a sign to us that the limit of God's forbearance is reached, that the measure of our nation's iniquity is full" (5T 451).

What will be the result of this national apostasy?

"A time is coming when the law of God is, in a special sense, to be made void in our land. The rulers of our nation will, by legislative enactments, enforce the Sunday law, and thus God's people be brought into great peril. When our nation, in its legislative councils, shall enact laws to bind the consciences of men in regard to their religious privileges, enforcing Sunday observance, and bringing oppressive power to bear against those who keep the seventh-day Sabbath, the law of God will, to all intents and purposes, be made void in our land; and national apostasy will be followed by national ruin" (RH Dec. 18, 1888; 7BC 977).

"It is at the time of the national apostasy, when acting on the policy of Satan, the rulers of the land will rank themselves on the side of the man of sin—it is then the measure of guilt is full; the national apostasy is the signal for national ruin" (GCB 1891, p. 259).

"The result of this apostasy will be national ruin" (RH May 2, 1893).

"Protestants will work upon the rulers of the land to make laws to restore the lost ascendancy of the man of sin, who sits in the temple of God, showing himself that he is God. Roman Catholic principles will be taken under the care and protection of the state. This national apostasy will speedily be followed by national ruin. . . . The Protestant governments will reach a strange pass. They will be converted to the world. They will also in their separation from God, work to make falsehood and apostasy from God the law of the nation" (RH June 15, 1897).

"When Protestant churches shall unite with the secular power to sustain a false religion, for opposing which their ancestors endured the fiercest persecution, then will the papal sabbath be enforced by the combined authority of church and state. There will be a national apostasy, which will end only in national ruin" (Ev 235 [1899]).

"When Protestant churches shall seek the support of the secular power, thus following the example of that apostate church, for opposing which their ancestors endured the fiercest persecution, then will there be a national apostasy which will end only in national ruin" (4SP 410 [1884]; ST July 4, 1899).

"When the Protestant churches shall unite with the secular power to sustain a false religion. . . ; when the state shall use its power to enforce the decrees and sustain the institutions of the church—then will Protestant America have formed an image to the papacy, and there will be a national apostasy which will end only in national ruin" (ST Mar. 22, 1910; 7BC 976).

How does Protestant America form an image of the beast?

"When the leading churches of the United States, uniting upon such points of doctrine as are held by them in common, shall influence the state to enforce their decrees and to sustain their institutions, then Protestant America will have formed an image of the Roman hierarchy, and the infliction of civil penalties upon dissenters will inevitably result" (GC 445 [see also 4SP 278]).

"In the very act of enforcing a religious duty by secular power, the churches would themselves form an image to the beast; hence the enforcement of Sundaykeeping in the United States would be an enforcement of the worship of the beast and his image" (GC 449).

Will the enforcement of Sundaykeeping (the forming of an image to the beast) in the United States follow or precede the close of probation?

"The Lord has shown me clearly that the image of the beast will be formed before probation closes; for it is to be the great test for the people of God. . . . This is the test that the people of God must have before they are sealed" (7BC 976).

"By the decree enforcing the institution of the papacy in violation of the law of God, our nation will disconnect herself fully from righteousness. When Protestantism shall stretch her hand across the gulf to grasp the hand of the Roman power, when she shall reach over the abyss to clasp hands with spiritualism, when, under the influence of this threefold union, our country shall repudiate every principle of its Constitution as a Protestant and republican government, and shall make provision for the propagation of papal falsehoods and delusions, then we may know that the time has come for the marvelous working of Satan and that the end is near.

"As the approach of the Roman armies was a sign to the disciples of the impending destruction of Jerusalem, so may this apostasy be a sign to us that the limit of God's forbearance is reached, that the measure of our nation's iniquity is full, and that the angel of mercy is about to take her flight, never to return" (5T 451).

"Anna's visions place the forming of the image of the beast after probation closes. This is not so. You claim to believe the testimonies; let them set you right on this point. The Lord has shown me clearly that the image of the beast will be formed before probation closes; for it is to be the great test for the people of God, by which their eternal destiny will be decided" (2SM 81).

In view of the anticipated Sunday legislation, what are city-dwelling Adventists urged to do as soon as possible?

"He wants us to live where we can have elbow room. His people are not to crowd into the cities. He wants them to take their families out of the cities, that they may better prepare for eternal life. In a little while they will have to leave the cities. . . . Get out of the cities as soon as possible" (*ibid.* 356).

"A crisis is soon to come in regard to the observance of Sunday. . . . If in the providence of God we can secure places away from the cities, the Lord would have us do this. There are troublous times before us. . . . I see the necessity of making haste to get all things ready for the crisis" (*ibid.* 359).

What warning will Sunday laws be to Adventists who still remain in the big cities?

"As the siege of Jerusalem by the Roman armies was the signal for flight to the Judean Christians, so the assumption of power on the part of our nation in the decree enforcing the papal sabbath will be a warning to us. It will then be time to leave the large cities, preparatory to leaving the smaller ones for retired homes in secluded places among the mountains" (5T 464, 465).

How are we to spend Sundays after the Sunday laws have been passed?

"Seventh-day Adventists were to show their wisdom by refraining from their ordinary work on that day, devoting it to missionary effort.

"To defy the Sunday laws will but strengthen in their persecution the religious zealots who are seeking to enforce them. Give them no occasion to call you lawbreakers. . . . One does not receive the mark of the beast because he shows that he realizes the wisdom of keeping the peace by refraining from work that gives offense. . . .

"Whenever it is possible, let religious services be held on Sunday. . . . Let the teachers in our schools devote Sunday to missionary effort" (9T 232, 233).

"Make no demonstration on Sunday in defiance of law" (*ibid. 235*).

"At one time those in charge of our school at Avondale inquired of me, saying: 'What shall we do? The officers of the law have been commissioned to arrest those working on Sunday.' I replied: 'It will be very easy to avoid that difficulty. Give Sunday to the Lord as a day for doing missionary work. Take the students out to hold meetings in different places, and to do medical missionary work. They will find the people at home and will have a splendid opportunity to present the truth. This way of spending Sunday is always acceptable to the Lord' " (*ibid. 238*).

"While we were living at Cooranbong, where the Avondale school is established," "the Sunday labor question came up for consideration. It seemed as if the lines were soon to be drawn so tightly about us that we should not be able to work on Sunday. Our school was situated in the heart of the woods, far from any village or railway station. No one was living near enough to be disturbed in any way by anything we might do. Nevertheless we were watched. The officers were urged to observe what we were doing on the school premises; and they did come, but they did not appear to notice those who were at work. Their confidence and respect for our people had been so won by the work we had done for the sick in that community that they did not wish to interfere with our harmless labor on Sunday.

"At another time when our brethren were threatened with persecution, and were questioning in regard to what they should do, I gave the same advice that I had given in answer to the question concerning the use of Sunday for games. I said, 'Employ Sunday in doing missionary work for God. Teachers, go with your students.'. . .

"Let the teachers in our schools devote Sunday to missionary effort" (CT 549-551).

What should be our attitude today? How should we work and pray?

"We are not doing the will of God if we sit in quietude, doing nothing to preserve liberty of conscience. Fervent, effectual prayer should be ascending to heaven that this calamity may be deferred until we can accomplish the work which has so long been neglected. Let there be most earnest prayer, and then let us work in harmony with our prayers. It may appear that Satan is triumphant and that truth is overborne with falsehood and error. . . . But God would have us recall His dealings with His people in the past to save them from their enemies. He has always chosen extremities, when there seemed no possible chance for deliverance from Satan's workings, for the manifestation of His power. Man's necessity is God's opportunity" (5T 714).

"We should diligently study the Word of God, and pray in faith that God will restrain the powers of darkness; for as yet the message has gone to comparatively few, and the world is to be lightened with its glory. The present truth—the commandments of God and the faith of Jesus—has not yet been sounded as it must be. . . . We must take a firm stand that we will not reverence the first day of the week as the Sabbath" (RH Extra Dec. 24, 1889).

"We have been looking many years for a Sunday law to be enacted in our land; and now that the movement is right upon us, we ask, What are our people going to do in the matter? . . . We should especially seek God for grace and power to be given His people now. God lives; and we do not believe that the time has fully come when He would have our liberties restricted. The prophet saw 'four angels standing on the four corners of the earth, holding the four winds of the earth, that the wind should not blow on the earth, nor on the sea, nor on any tree.' Another angel ascending from the east cried to them, saying, 'Hurt not the earth, neither the sea, nor the trees, till we have sealed the servants of our God in their foreheads.' This points out the work we now have to do, which is to cry to God for the angels to hold the four winds until missionaries shall be sent to all parts of the world, and shall have proclaimed the warning against disobeying the law of Jehovah" (RH Extra Dec. 11, 1888).

"A vast responsibility is devolving upon men and women of prayer throughout the land, to petition that God may sweep back this cloud of evil, and give a few more years of grace to work for the Master" *(ibid.)*.

"We see that those who are now keeping the commandments of God need to bestir themselves, that they may obtain the special help which God alone can give them. They should work more earnestly to delay as long as possible the threatened calamity" (RH Dec. 18, 1888).

"If they do nothing to disabuse the minds of the people, and through ignorance of the truth our legislatures should abjure the principles of Protestantism, and give countenance and support to the Roman fallacy, the spurious sabbath, God will hold His people, who have had great light, responsible for their lack of diligence and faithfulness. But if the subject of religious legislation is judiciously and intelligently laid before the people, and they see that through Sunday enforcement to Roman apostasy would be reenacted by the Christian world, and that the tyranny of past ages would be repeated, then whatever comes, we shall have done our duty" (RH Extra Dec. 24, 1889).

"Let not the commandment-keeping people of God be silent at this time, as though we gracefully accepted the situation. There is the prospect before us of waging a continuous war, at the risk of imprisonment, of losing property and even life itself, to defend the law of God, which is being made void by the laws of men" (RH Jan. 1, 1889 [7BC 975]).

"I do hope that the trumpet will give a certain sound in regard to this Sunday-law movement. I think that it would be best if in our papers the subject of the perpetuity of the law of God were made a specialty. . . . We should now be doing our very best to defeat this Sunday law" (CW 97, 98 [1906]).

"There are many who are at ease, who are, as it were, asleep. They say, 'If prophecy has foretold the enforcement of Sunday observance, the law will surely be enacted;' and having come to this conclusion, they sit down in calm expectation of the event, comforting themselves with the thought that God will protect His people in the day of trouble. But God will not save us if we make no effort to do the work He has committed to our charge" (RH Extra Dec. 24, 1889).

"Those who have been warned of the events before them are not to sit in calm expectation of the coming storm, comforting themselves that the Lord will shelter His faithful ones in the day of trouble. We are to be as men waiting for their Lord, not in idle expectancy, but in earnest work, with unwavering faith. It is no time now to allow our minds to be engrossed with things of minor importance. . . . The Sunday movement is now making its way in darkness. The leaders are concealing the true issue, and many who unite in the movement do not themselves see whither the undercurrent is tending. Its professions are mild, and apparently Christian; but when it shall speak, it will reveal the spirit of the dragon. It is our duty to do all in our power to avert the threatened danger. We should endeavor to disarm prejudice by placing ourselves in a proper light before the people. We should bring before them the real question at issue, thus interposing the most effectual protest against measures to restrict liberty of conscience. We should search the Scriptures, and be able to give the reason for our faith" (RH Extra Dec. 11, 1888).

Patriarchs and Prophets, Daniel and the Revelation, and *The Great Controversy* are needed now as never before. They should be widely circulated because the truths they emphasize will open many blind eyes. . . . Many of our people have been blind to the importance of the very books that were most needed. Had tact and skill then been shown in the sale of these books, the Sunday-law movement would not be where it is today" (CM 123 [RH Feb. 16, 1905]).

"We cannot labor to please men who will use their influence to repress religious liberty, and to set in operation oppressive measures to lead or compel their fellow men to keep Sunday as the Sabbath. The first day of the week is not a day to be reverenced. It is a spurious sabbath, and the members of the Lord's family cannot participate with the men who exalt this day, and violate the law of God by trampling upon His Sabbath. The people of God are not to vote to place such men in office; for when they do this, they are partakers with them of the sins which they commit while in office" (FE 475 [GW 391, 392]).

CHAPTER 4

THE UNIVERSAL SUNDAY LAW

What does the Bible say about the worldwide resurgence of Roman Catholic influence before the end of time?

Rev. 13:3, 8.

What favored nation will lead out in the enforcement of Sunday observance?

"This very class put forth the claim that the fast-spreading corruption is largely attributable to the desecration of the so-called 'Christian sabbath,' and that the enforcement of Sunday observance would greatly improve the morals of society. This claim is especially urged in America, where the doctrine of the true Sabbath has been most widely preached" (GC 587).

"Foreign nations will follow the example of the United States. Though she leads out, yet the same crisis will come upon our people in all parts of the world" (6T 395).

How many nations will follow the example of the United States?

"As America, the land of religious liberty, shall unite with the papacy in forcing the conscience and compelling men to honor the false sabbath, the people of every country on the globe will be led to follow her example" (*ibid.* 18).

"The Sabbath question is to be the issue in the great final conflict in which all the world will act a part" (6T 352).

What one world religion, in particular, is concerned with enforcing Sunday observance?

"As the Sabbath has become the special point of controversy throughout Christendom, and religious and secular authorities have combined to enforce the observance of the Sunday, the persistent refusal of a small minority to yield to the popular demand will make them objects of universal execration" (GC 615).

"All Christendom will be divided into two great classes—those who keep the commandments of God and the faith of Jesus, and those who worship the beast and his image and receive his mark" (*ibid.* 450 [9T 16; 2SM 55]).

What will happen to Seventh-day Adventists who cannot comply with the Sunday law?

"The decree enforcing the worship of this day is to go forth to all the world. . . . Trial and persecution will come to all who, in obedience to the Word of God, refuse to worship this false sabbath" (7BC 976).

"The whole world is to be stirred with enmity against Seventh-day Adventists, because they will not yield homage to the papacy, by honoring Sunday, the institution of this antichristian power. It is the purpose of Satan to cause them to be blotted from the earth, in order that his supremacy of the world may not be disputed" (TM 37 [RH Aug. 22, 1893]).

What effect will the false revival have upon most nominal Christians?

"They declared that they had the truth, that miracles were among them, . . . that great power and signs and wonders were performed among them, and that this was the temporal millennium that they had been expecting so long. The whole world was converted and in harmony with the Sunday law" (21MR 325, 326).

What two opposing marks will be received by the two groups of people in the world when Sundaykeeping is enforced by law?

"While the observance of the false sabbath in compliance with the law of the state, contrary to the fourth commandment, will be an avowal of allegiance to a power that is in opposition to God, the keeping of the true Sabbath, in obedience to God's law, is an evidence of loyalty to the Creator. While one class, by accepting the sign of submission to earthly powers, receive the mark of the beast, the other, choosing the token of allegiance to divine authority, receive the seal of God" (GC 605).

"Fearful is the issue to which the world is to be brought. The powers of earth, uniting to war against the commandments of God, will decree that 'all, both small and great, rich and poor, free and bond' (Rev. 13:16), shall conform to the customs of the church by the observance of the false sabbath. All who refuse compliance will be visited with civil penalties, and it will finally be declared that they are deserving of death. On the other hand, the law of God enjoining the Creator's rest day demands obedience and threatens wrath against all who transgress its precepts.

"With the issue thus clearly brought before him, whoever shall trample upon God's law to obey a human enactment receives the mark of the beast" (*ibid.* 604).

What relationship does the universal Sunday law bear to the close of probation?

"God gives nations a certain time of probation" (4BC 1143).

"With unerring accuracy the Infinite One still keeps an account with all nations. While His mercy is tendered, with calls to repentance, this account will remain open; but when the figures reach a certain amount which God has fixed, the ministry of His wrath commences. The account is closed. Divine patience ceases. There is no more pleading of mercy in their behalf" (5T 208).

"God keeps a record with the nations: the figures are swelling against them in the books of heaven; and when it shall have become a law that the transgression of the first day of the week shall be met with punishment, then their cup will be full" (7BC 910).

"When the accumulated figures in heaven's record books shall mark the sum of transgression complete, wrath will come, unmixed with mercy, and then it will be seen what a tremendous thing it is to have worn out the divine patience. This crisis will be reached when the nations shall unite in making void God's law" (5T 524).

"The substitution of the false for the true is the last act in the drama. When this substitution becomes universal, God will reveal Himself. When the laws of men are exalted above the laws of God, when the powers of this earth try to force men to keep the first day of the week, know that the time has come for God to work. He will arise in His majesty, and will shake terribly the earth. He will come out of His place to punish the inhabitants of the world for their iniquity" (7BC 980).

Do all Seventh-day Adventists believe that the universal Sunday law will be passed before probation's close?

No, they do not. Some students of the Bible and the Spirit of Prophecy expect that Sunday legislation will not become universal until some time after the close of probation.

The quotations listed under the previous question (see p. 37) are interpreted in this way. Another supporting statement used is: "When Jesus leaves the most holy, His restraining Spirit is withdrawn from rulers and people.

They are left to the control of evil angels. Then such laws will be made by the counsel and direction of Satan, that unless time should be very short, no flesh could be saved" (1T 204).

THE LITTLE TIME OF TROUBLE

(Before Probation's Close)

What has often been the lot of God's children in the past?

2 Tim. 3:12; John 15:20; 16:2; Dan. 7:25; Rev. 13:7.

Has Satan changed, or is he still a persecutor?

Rev. 13:15-17.

What specific perplexities will Satan bring upon the saints in the future?

Rev. 13:15-17.

When do these troubles begin, in relationship to the close of probation?

"I saw that God had children who do not see and keep the Sabbath. They have not rejected the light upon it. And at the commencement of the time of trouble, we were filled with the Holy Ghost as we went forth and proclaimed the Sabbath more fully" (EW 33).

" 'The commencement of the time of trouble,' here mentioned, does not refer to the time when the plagues shall begin to be poured out, but to a short period just before they are poured out, while Christ is in the sanctuary" (*ibid.* 85).

What is one of the principal causes of this time of trouble?

"God's Sabbath will be trampled under foot, and a false

sabbath will be exalted. In a Sunday law there is possibility for great suffering to those who observe the seventh day. The working out of Satan's plans will bring persecution to the people of God. But the faithful servants of God need not fear the outcome of the conflict" (2SM 375).

"If popery or its principles shall again be legislated into power, the fires of persecution will be rekindled against those who will not sacrifice conscience and the truth in deference to popular errors. This evil is on the point of realization" (5T 712).

Will God's people be persecuted for Sunday-breaking or for Sabbathkeeping?

"The Protestant world today see in the little company keeping the Sabbath a Mordecai in the gate. His character and conduct, expressing reverence for the law of God, are a constant rebuke to those who have cast off the fear of the Lord and are trampling upon His Sabbath; the unwelcome intruder must by some means be put out of the way" (ibid. 450).

"God's people will feel the hand of persecution because they keep holy the seventh day" (7BC 975 [9T 229]).

"Let there be a revival of the faith and power of the early church, and the spirit of persecution will be revived, and the fires of persecution will be rekindled" (GC 48).

How bitter will hatred of Seventh-day Adventists become?

"Those who honor the Bible Sabbath will be denounced as enemies of law and order, as breaking down the moral restraints of society, causing anarchy and corruption, and calling down the judgments of God upon the earth. Their conscientious scruples will be pronounced obstinacy, stubbornness, and contempt of authority. They will be accused of disaffection toward the government. Ministers who deny the obligation of the divine law will present from the pulpit the duty of yielding obedience to the civil authorities as ordained of God. In legislative halls and courts of justice, commandment keepers will be misrepresented and condemned. A false coloring will be given to their words; the worst construction will be put upon their motives" (GC 592 [see also PK 183, 184]).

"Before the warfare shall be ended and the victory won, we as a people are to experience trials similar to those of Paul. We shall encounter the same hardness of heart, the same cruel determination, the same unyielding hatred. . . . Persecution will again be kindled against those who are true to God; their motives will be impugned, their best efforts misinterpreted, their names cast out as evil. . . . God would have His people prepared for the soon-coming crisis. Prepared or unprepared, we must all meet it" (SLP 251, 252).

"There will come a time when, because of our advocacy of Bible truth, we shall be treated as traitors" (6T 394).

"Wealth, genius, education, will combine to cover them with contempt. Persecuting rulers, ministers, and church members will conspire against them. With voice and pen, by boasts, threats, and ridicule, they will seek to overthrow their faith" (5T 450).

What organizations will make it extremely difficult for Adventists to continue their work in the cities?

"The trades unions will be one of the agencies that will bring upon this earth a time of trouble such as has not been since the world began" (2SM 142).

"Because of these unions and confederacies, it will soon be very difficult for our institutions to carry on their work in the cities. My warning is: Keep out of the cities. Build no sanitariums in the cities" (*ibid.* 142).

"A few men will combine to grasp all the means to be obtained in certain lines of business. Trades unions will be formed, and those who refuse to join these unions will be marked men" (*ibid.* 142).

"The time is fast coming when the controlling power of the labor unions will be very oppressive. Again and again the Lord has instructed that our people are to take their families away from the cities, into the country, where they can raise their own provisions; for in the future the problem of buying and selling will be a very serious one" (*ibid.* 141).

As time progresses, what official decree will go forth concerning buying and selling?

"In the last great conflict of the controversy with Satan those who are loyal to God will see every earthly support cut off. Because they refuse to break His law in obedience to earthly powers, they will be forbidden to buy or sell" (DA 121, 122).

"Satan says, . . . 'For fear of wanting food and clothing, they will join with the world in transgressing God's law. The earth will be wholly under my dominion'" (PK 183, 184 [see also 5T 152]).

"Hoarded wealth will soon be worthless. When the decree shall go forth that none shall buy or sell except they have the mark of the beast, very much means will be of no avail. God calls for us now to do all in our power to send forth the warning to the world" (RH Mar. 21, 1878).

"The time is coming when we cannot sell at any price. The decree will soon go forth prohibiting men to buy or sell of any man save him that hath the mark of the beast. We came near having this realized in California a short time since; but this was only the threatening of the blowing of the four winds. As yet they are held by the four angels. We are not just ready. There is a work yet to be done, and then the angels will be bidden to let go, that the four winds may blow upon the earth. That will be a decisive time for God's children, a time of trouble such as never was since there was a nation. Now is our opportunity to work" (5T 152).

What additional law will be enacted before the close of probation?

"Wonderful events are soon to open before the world. The end of all things is at hand. The time of trouble is about to come upon the people of God. Then it is that the decree will go forth forbidding those who keep the Sabbath of the Lord to buy or sell, and threatening them with punishment, and even death, if they do not observe the first day of the week as the Sabbath.

" 'And at that time shall Michael stand up, the great prince which standeth for the children of thy people: and there shall be a time of trouble, such as never was since there was a nation even to that same time' " (RH Nov. 19, 1908).

How will some young people be treated by their own parents?

"Conscientious obedience to the Word of God will be treated as rebellion. Blinded by Satan, the parent will exercise harshness and severity toward the believing child; the master or mistress will oppress the commandment-keeping servant. Affection will be alienated; children will be disinherited and driven from home" (GC 608).

How will some be dealt with by judicial courts?

"And all who prove their loyalty by obedience to the law of Jehovah must be prepared to be arrested, to be brought before councils that have not for their standard the high and holy law of God" (RH Dec. 26, 1899 [7BC 977]).

"The tender mercies of this power will be displayed in prison cells and dungeons. Already preparations are advancing, and movements are in progress, which will result in making an image to the beast" (RH Apr. 23, 1889).

"As the defenders of truth refuse to honor the Sunday-sabbath, some of them will be thrust into prison, some will be exiled, some will be treated as slaves. To human wisdom all this now seems impossible; but as the restraining Spirit of God shall be withdrawn from men, and they shall be under the control of Satan, who hates the divine precepts, there will be strange developments. The heart can be very cruel when God's fear and love are removed" (GC 608).

Is it possible that some may make the supreme sacrifice?

"There is a prospect before us of a continued struggle, at the risk of imprisonment, loss of property, and even of life itself, to defend the law of God" (5T 712).

"As he influenced the heathen nations to destroy Israel, so in the near future he will stir up the wicked powers of earth to destroy the people of God. Men will be required to render obedience to human edicts in violation of the divine law.

Will those who are condemned for their faith be afraid of the prison cell or even of death itself?

"If we are called to suffer for Christ's sake, we shall be able to go to prison trusting in Him as a little child trusts in its parents. Now is the time to cultivate faith in God" (OHC 357).

"We are not to have the courage and fortitude of martyrs of old until brought into the position they were in. . . .

Should there be a return of persecution there would be grace given to arouse every energy of the soul to show a true heroism" (*ibid.* 125).

"The disciples were not endowed with the courage and fortitude of the martyrs until such grace was needed" (DA 354).

"When for the truth's sake the believer stands at the bar of the unrighteous tribunals, Christ stands by his side. . . . When one is incarcerated in prison walls, Christ ravishes the heart with His love. When one suffers death for His sake, Christ says, 'I am he that liveth, and was dead; and, behold, I am alive for evermore, . . . and have the keys of hell and of death' (Rev. 1:18). The life that is sacrificed for Me is preserved unto eternal glory" (DA 669).

Who will be the devil's most efficient agents in the misrepresentation and accusation of Adventists?

"Men of talent and pleasing address, who once rejoiced in the truth, employ their powers to deceive and mislead souls. They become the most bitter enemies of their former brethren. When Sabbathkeepers are brought before the courts to answer for their faith, these apostates are the most efficient agents of Satan to misrepresent and accuse them, and by false reports and insinuations to stir up the rulers against them" (GC 608).

What two powerful Christian groups will unite to persecute the advocates of truth?

"The professed Protestant world will form a confederacy with the man of sin. . . . The Scriptures teach that popery is to regain its lost supremacy, and that the fires of persecution will be rekindled" (7BC 975).

"Many will plead that there is no prospect that popery will ever be revived. If it shall regain its lost ascendancy, it will be by Protestantism's giving it the right hand of fellowship. If it shall be legislated into power by the concessions of time-serving men, the fires of persecution will be rekindled against those who will not sacrifice conscience and the truth for the errors of the papacy. Once let the minds of the Christian world be turned away from God; let His law be dishonored and His holy day trampled upon, and they will be ready to take any step where Satan may lead the way" (RH Jan. 1, 1889).

"The church appeals to the strong arm of civil power, and, in this work, papists and Protestants unite" (GC 607).

"All who will not bow to the decree of the national councils and obey the national laws to exalt the sabbath instituted by the man of sin, to the disregard of God's holy day, will feel, not the oppressive power of popery alone, but of the Protestant world, the image of the beast" (2SM 380).

"The popular ministry, like the Pharisees of old, filled with anger as their authority is questioned, will denounce the message as of Satan and stir up the sin-loving multitudes to revile and persecute those who proclaim it" (GC 607).

"Protestants are working in disguise to bring Sunday to the front, as did the Romanists. Throughout the land the papacy is piling up her lofty and massive structures, in the secret recesses of which her former persecutions are to be repeated" (5T 449, 450 [see also GC 581]).

Will this persecution be uniform everywhere?

"As long as the message of mercy is to be given to the world, there will be a call for effort in behalf of other institutions and enterprises similar to that for the relief of our schools. And as long as probation continues, there will be opportunity for the canvasser to work. When the religious denominations unite with the papacy to oppress God's people, places where there is religious freedom will be opened by evangelistic canvassing. If in one place the persecution becomes severe, let the workers do as Christ has directed. 'When they persecute you in this city, flee ye into another.' If persecution comes there, go to still another place. God will lead His people, making them a blessing in many places. Were it not for persecution they would not be so widely scattered abroad to proclaim the truth" (6T 478).

How will unsanctified church members be affected by the storm of ridicule, trial, and contempt?

"As the storm approaches, a large class who have professed faith in the third angel's message, but have not been sanctified through obedience to the truth, abandon their position and join the ranks of the opposition. By uniting with the world and partaking of its spirit, they have come to view matters in nearly the same light; and when the test is brought, they are prepared to choose the easy, popular side" (GC 608).

How will the "true sheep" react when persecution comes?

"When the storm of persecution really breaks upon us, the true sheep will hear the true Shepherd's voice. Self-denying efforts will be put forth to save the lost, and many who have strayed from the fold will come back to follow the great Shepherd. The people of God will draw together and present to the enemy a united front. In view of the common peril, strife for supremacy will cease; there will be no disputing as to who shall be accounted greatest" (6T 401).

What mighty demonstration of the power of God will be seen throughout the world after persecution begins?

"The love of Christ, the love of our brethren, will testify to the world that we have been with Jesus and learned of Him. Then will the message of the third angel swell to a loud cry, and the whole earth will be lightened with the glory of the Lord" *(ibid.)*.

What should be our present attitude and conduct as we anticipate trouble ahead?

"Over and over the message has been given to me that we are not to say one word, not to publish one sentence, especially by way of personalities, unless positively essential in vindicating the truth, that will stir up our enemies against us and arouse their passions to a white heat. Our work will soon be closed up, and soon the time of trouble, such as never was, will come upon us, of which we have but little idea" (9T 241).

"Let everyone bear in mind that we are in no case to invite persecution. We are not to use harsh and cutting words. Keep them out of every article written, drop them out of every address given. Let the Word of God do the cutting, the rebuking; let finite men hide and abide in Jesus Christ. . . .

"There is to be a time of trouble such as never was since there was a nation" *(ibid.* 244).

"The time is right upon us when persecution will come to those who proclaim the truth. The outlook is not flattering; but, notwithstanding this, let us not give up our efforts to save those ready to perish, for whose ransom the Prince of heaven offered up His precious life. When one means fails, try another. Our efforts must not be dead and lifeless. As long as life is spared, let us work for God" *(ibid.* 227).

THE MIGHTY SIFTING

What is the Bible teaching on the subject of the perseverance of the saints (once saved, always saved)? Is it possible for a genuine Christian to lose his or her love for God?

Matt. 24:13; 13:18-23; 1 Cor. 9:27; 10:12; Heb. 6:4-6; Eze. 18:24; 2 Peter 2:20, 21.

Does the Bible describe the apostasy of any particular individuals who once had God's approval?

Eze. 28:15; 2 Peter 2:4; 1 Sam. 10:9; 28:15.

Is apostatizing (the "shaking" of members out of God's church) limited to bygone centuries only?

"The mighty shaking has commenced and will go on, and all will be shaken out who are not willing to take a bold and unyielding stand for the truth and to sacrifice for God and His cause. The angel said, 'Think ye that any will be compelled to sacrifice? No, no. It must be a freewill offering'" (EW 50, 51 [1851]).

"I saw that we are now in the shaking time. Satan is working with all his power to wrest souls from the hand of Christ" (1T 429 [1864]).

"God is now sifting His people, testing their purposes and their motives. Many will be but as chaff—no wheat, no value in them" (4T 51 [1876]).

"We are in the shaking time, the time when everything that can be shaken will be shaken. The Lord will not excuse those who know the truth if they do not in word and deed obey His commands" (6T 332 [1900]).

"Even in our day there have been and will continue to be entire families who have once rejoiced in the truth, but who will lose faith because of calumnies and falsehoods brought to them in regard to those whom they have loved and with whom they have had sweet counsel. They opened their hearts to the sowing of tares; the tares sprang up among the wheat; they strengthened; the crop of wheat became less and less; and the precious truth lost its power to them" (TM 411).

What experience of the near future will greatly increase the number of apostasies from the Seventh-day Adventist Church?

"The time is not far distant when the test will come to every soul. The mark of the beast will be urged upon us. Those who have step by step yielded to worldly demands and conformed to worldly customs will not find it a hard matter to yield to the powers that be, rather than subject themselves to derision, insult, threatened imprisonment, and death. The contest is between the commandments of God and the commandments of men. In this time the gold will be separated from the dross in the church" (5T 81).

"The work which the church has failed to do in a time of peace and prosperity she will have to do in a terrible crisis under most discouraging, forbidding circumstances. . . . And at that time the superficial, conservative class, whose influence has steadily retarded the progress of the work, will renounce the faith" (5T 463).

"As trials thicken around us, both separation and unity will be seen in our ranks. Some who are now ready to take up weapons of warfare will in times of real peril make it manifest that they have not built upon the solid rock; they will yield to temptation. Those who have had great light and precious privileges, but have not improved them, will, under one pretext or another, go out from us" (6T 400).

"In the absence of the persecution there have drifted into our ranks men who appear sound and their Christianity unquestionable, but who, if persecution should arise, would go out from us" (Ev 360).

Besides persecution, what other causes are there for the "shaking" of God's people?

"I asked the meaning of the shaking I had seen and was shown that it would be caused by the straight testimony called forth by the counsel of the True Witness to the Laodiceans. This will have its effect upon the heart of the receiver, and will lead him to exalt the standard and pour forth the straight truth. Some will not bear this straight testimony. They will rise up against it, and this is what will cause a shaking among God's people" (EW 270).

"God's Spirit has illuminated every page of Holy Writ, but there are those upon whom it makes little impression, because it is imperfectly understood. When the shaking comes, by the introduction of false theories, these surface readers, anchored nowhere, are like shifting sand. They slide into any position to suit the tenor of their feelings of bitterness" (TM 112).

"Not having received the love of the truth, they will be taken in the delusions of the enemy; they will give heed to seducing spirits and doctrines of devils, and will depart from the faith" (6T 401).

What expression does Mrs. White use to describe this experience?

"In the mighty sifting soon to take place we shall be better able to measure the strength of Israel. The signs reveal that the time is near when the Lord will manifest that His fan is in His hand, and He will thoroughly purge His floor" (5T 80).

Has our entire church membership ever been composed of true Christians?

"From what has been shown me, there are not more than half of the young who profess religion and the truth who have been truly converted" (1T 158 [MYP 131] [1857]).

"Names are registered upon the church books upon earth, but not in the book of life. I saw that there is not one in twenty of the youth who knows what experimental religion is" (1T 504 [MYP 384] [1867]).

"In the last vision given me, I was shown the startling fact that but a small portion of those who now profess the truth will be sanctified by it and be saved" (1T 608 [1867]).

"I have stated before them that, from what was shown me, but a small number of those now professing to believe the truth would eventually be saved" (2T 445 [1870]).

"I tell you not a few ministers who stand before the people to explain the Scriptures are defiled. Their hearts are corrupt, their hands unclean" (5T 78 [1882]).

"It is a solemn statement that I make to the church, that not one in twenty whose names are registered upon the church books are prepared to close their earthly history" (ChS 41 [1893]).

In the days of ease and prosperity that we are now enjoying, what can we expect to develop in our church?

"Prosperity multiplies a mass of professors. Adversity purges them out of the church" (4T 89).

"Divisions will come in the church. Two parties will be developed. The wheat and tares grow up together for the harvest" (2SM 114).

When the "mighty sifting" takes place, what will become of the unconsecrated members of our church?

"When the day comes when the law of God is made void, and the church is sifted by the fiery trials that are to try all that live upon the earth, a great proportion of those who are supposed to be genuine will give heed to seducing spirits, and will turn traitors and betray sacred trusts. They will prove our very worst persecutors" (6BC 1065).

"Many a star that we have admired for its brilliance will then go out in darkness" (PK 188 [see also 5T 81]).

"Chaff like a cloud will be borne away on the wind, even from places where we see only floors of rich wheat" (5T 81).

"The shaking of God blows away multitudes like dry leaves" (4T 89).

"In the last solemn work few great men will be engaged" (5T 80).

What percentage of our Seventh-day Adventist Church membership will apostatize?

"Soon God's people will be tested by fiery trials, and the great proportion of those who now appear to be genuine and true will prove to be base metal" (*ibid.* 136).

"To stand in defense of truth and righteousness when the majority forsake us, to fight the battles of the Lord when champions are few—this will be our test. At this time we must gather warmth from the coldness of others, courage from their cowardice, and loyalty from their treason" (*ibid.* 136).

"When the law of God is made void, the church will be sifted by fiery trials, and a larger proportion than we now anticipate will give heed to seducing spirits and doctrines of devils" (2SM 368 [Ev 361]).

Will all unconsecrated Seventh-day Adventists be shaken out of the church in this period of trial before probation's close?

"Those professed believers who come up to the time of trouble unprepared will, in their despair, confess their sins before all in words of burning anguish, while the wicked exult over their distress. The case of all such is hopeless. When Christ stands up, and leaves the Most Holy Place, then the time of trouble commences, and the case of every soul is decided" (3SG 134).

Should our people be constantly reminded that persecution is coming and that large numbers will apostatize?

"There is a time of trouble coming to the people of God, but we are not to keep that constantly before the people, and rein them up to have a time of trouble beforehand. There is to be a shaking among God's people; but this is not the present truth to carry to the churches" (1SM 180 [2SM 13]).

When the majority of our members withdraw, will the Seventh-day Adventist Church collapse?

"The church may appear as about to fall, but it does not fall. It remains, while the sinners in Zion will be sifted out—the chaff separated from the precious wheat. This is a terrible ordeal, but nevertheless it must take place" (2SM 380).

"The church is the depositary of the wealth of the riches of the grace of Christ, and through the church eventually will be made manifest the final and full display of the love of God to the world that is to be lightened with its glory" (TM 50).

"The bulwarks of Satan will never triumph. Victory will attend the third angel's message. As the Captain of the Lord's host tore down the walls of Jericho, so will the

Lord's commandment-keeping people triumph, and all opposing elements be defeated" (*ibid.* 410).

How will this "terrible ordeal" affect the outlook and attitude of the loyal Adventists who remain in the church?

"Let opposition arise, let bigotry and intolerance again bear sway, let persecution be kindled, and the halfhearted and hypocritical will waver and yield the faith; but the true Christian will stand firm as a rock, his faith stronger, his hope brighter, than in days of prosperity" (GC 602).

"Amidst the deepening shadows of earth's last great crisis, God's light will shine brightest, and the song of hope and trust will be heard in clearest and loftiest strains" (Ed 166).

"When the storm of persecution really breaks upon us, the true sheep will hear the true Shepherd's voice. Self-denying efforts will be put forth to save the lost, and many who have strayed from the fold will come back to follow the great Shepherd. The people of God will draw together and present to the enemy a united front. In view of the common peril, strife for supremacy will cease; there will be no disputing as to who shall be accounted greatest. . . . Then will the message of the third angel swell to a loud cry, and the whole earth will be lightened with the glory of the Lord" (6T 401).

What do these immovable Adventists now have in their foreheads?

"Just as soon as the people of God are sealed in their foreheads—it is not any seal or mark that can be seen, but a settling into the truth, both intellectually and spiritually, so they cannot be moved—just as soon as God's people are sealed and prepared for the shaking, it will come.

Indeed, it has begun already; the judgments of God are now upon the land, to give us warning, that we may know what is coming" (4BC 1161).

As the message now swells to a loud cry, what will be the result?

"Standard after standard was left to trail in the dust as company after company from the Lord's army joined the foe and tribe after tribe from the ranks of the enemy united with the commandment-keeping people of God" (8T 41).

"The numbers of this company had lessened. Some had been shaken out and left by the way. The careless and indifferent, who did not join with those who prized victory and salvation enough to perseveringly plead and agonize for it, did not obtain it, and they were left behind in darkness, and their places were immediately filled by others taking hold of the truth and coming into the ranks" (EW 271 [see also 1T 182]).

"The Lord has faithful servants, who in the shaking, testing time will be disclosed to view. There are precious ones now hidden who have not bowed the knee to Baal. They have not had the light which has been shining in a concentrated blaze upon you. But it may be under a rough and uninviting exterior the pure brightness of a genuine Christian character will be revealed. In the daytime we look toward heaven but do not see the stars. They are there, fixed in the firmament, but the eye cannot distinguish them. In the night we behold their genuine luster" (5T 80, 81).

"Notwithstanding the agencies combined against the truth, a large number take their stand upon the Lord's side" (GC 612).

BEFORE RULERS AND KINGS

By what means has God at times brought the gospel to the attention of the great men of earth?

Matt. 10:17-20; Mark 13:9-11; Acts 5:21, 27; 25:22; Phil. 1:12, 13.

Before whom will God's people be privileged to bear witness of their faith in the near future?

"Many will have to stand in the legislative courts; some will have to stand before kings and before the learned of the earth, to answer for their faith" (OHC 355).

"The time is not far off when the people of God will be called upon to give their testimony before the rulers of the earth. Not one in twenty has a realization of what rapid strides we are making toward the great crisis in our history" (*ibid.* 355).

"They will have the privilege of bringing the light before those who are called the great men of the earth, and if you have studied the Bible, if you are ready to give an answer to every man that asketh you of the hope that is in you with meekness and fear, your enemies will not be able to gainsay your wisdom" (*ibid.* 355).

"Many will be called to speak before councils and in courts of justice, perhaps separately and alone. The experience which would have helped them in this emergency they have neglected to obtain, and their souls are burdened with remorse for wasted opportunities and neglected privileges" (5T 463).

Will we be tested as groups or as individuals?

"The members of the church will individually be tested and proved. They will be placed in circumstances where they will be forced to bear witness for the truth" *(ibid.)*.

"It does not seem possible to us now that any should have to stand alone; but if God has ever spoken by me, the time will come when we shall be brought before councils and before thousands for His name's sake, and each one will have to give the reason of his faith. Then will come the severest criticism upon every position that has been taken for the truth. We need, then, to study the Word of God, that we may know why we believe the doctrines we advocate" (RH Dec. 18, 1888 [see also 5T 717; Ev 69]).

Does this mean ministers only, or should every church member prepare to be publicly tested?

"Many will have to stand in the legislative courts; some will have to stand before kings and before the learned of the earth, to answer for their faith. . . . Let no one imagine that he has no need to study, because he is not to preach in the sacred desk. You know not what God may require of you" (OHC 355).

Are we all now ready to be cross-examined for our faith?

"I have been shown that many who profess to have a knowledge of present truth know not what they believe. They do not understand the evidences of their faith. They have no just appreciation of the work for the present time. When the time of trial shall come, there are men now preaching to others who will find, upon examining the positions they hold, that there are many things for which they can give no satisfactory reason. Until thus tested they knew not their great ignorance. And there are many in the church who take it for granted that they understand what they believe; but, until controversy arises, they do not know their own weakness. When separated from those of like faith and compelled to stand singly and alone to explain their belief, they will be surprised to see how confused are their ideas of what they had accepted as truth" (5T 707).

"Those who have only a superficial understanding of truth will not be able clearly to expound the Scriptures, and give definite reasons for their faith. They will become confused, and will not be workmen that need not to be ashamed" (OHC 355).

What should we be doing now in order to be ready when brought to trial for our faith?

"The servants of Christ are to prepare no set speech to present when brought to trial for their faith. Their preparation is to be made day by day, in treasuring up in their hearts the precious truths of God's Word, in feeding upon the teaching of Christ, and through prayer strengthening their faith; then, when [they are] brought into trial, the Holy Spirit will bring to their remembrance the very truths that will reach the hearts of those who shall come to hear. God will flash the knowledge obtained by diligent searching of the Scriptures into their memory at the very time when it is needed" (OHC 356 [see also CSW 41]).

"Our people need to understand the oracles of God; they need to have a systematic knowledge of the principles of revealed truth, which will fit them for what is coming upon the earth, and prevent them from being carried about by every wind of doctrine" (5T 273).

"Our people have been regarded as too insignificant to be worthy of notice, but a change will come. The Christian world is now making movements which will necessarily bring commandment-keeping people into prominence. . . .

Every position of our faith will be searched into; and if we are not thorough Bible students, established, strengthened, and settled, the wisdom of the world's great men will lead us astray (*ibid.* 546).

What is even more important than the ability to give a reason for our faith?

"The ability to give a reason for our faith is a good accomplishment, but if the truth does not go deeper than this, the soul will never be saved. The heart must be purified from all moral defilement" (OHC 142).

"You are now to get ready for the time of trial. Now you are to know whether your feet are planted on the Eternal Rock. You must have an individual experience, and not depend upon others for your light. When you are brought to the test, how do you know that you will not be alone, with no earthly friend at your side? Will you then be able to realize that Christ is your support?" (*ibid.* 356).

What is the purpose of these public trials?

"God means that testing truth shall be brought to the front and become a subject of examination and discussion, even if it is through the contempt placed upon it. The minds of the people must be agitated. Every controversy, every reproach, every slander, will be God's means of provoking inquiry and awakening minds that otherwise would slumber" (5T 453 [RH Extra Dec. 11, 1888]).

SATAN'S MIRACLES

Was spiritism a problem in Bible times?
Ex. 22:18; Lev. 20:6, 27; Deut. 18:9-12; Mark 5:1-18; 9:14-29; Acts 16:16-18.

How did Satan at times personate something or someone more attractive than himself?
Gen. 3:1-5; 1 Sam. 28:6-14.

Is he still capable of transforming himself into that which is desirable?
2 Cor. 11:13-15.

For what purpose will Satan perform miracles in the very last days of earth's history?
Rev. 16:13, 14; 13:13, 14; 2 Thess. 2:9, 10; Matt. 24:4, 24.

Where did modern spiritualism begin?
"I saw that the mysterious knocking in New York [Hydesville, New York, in 1848] and other places was the power of Satan, and that such things would be more and more common, clothed in a religious garb so as to lull the deceived to greater security and to draw the minds of God's people, if possible, to those things and cause them to doubt the teachings and power of the Holy Ghost" (EW 43).

"The mysterious rapping with which modern spiritualism began was not the result of human trickery or cunning, but was the direct work of evil angels" (GC 553).

In what way is spiritualism now changing its form?

"Spiritualism is now changing its form and, veiling some of its more objectionable features, is assuming a Christian guise. . . . While it formerly denounced Christ and the Bible, it now *professes* to accept both" (*ibid.* 557, 558).

What is Satan now making special preparation for?

"Satan has long been preparing for his final effort to deceive the world. . . . Little by little he has prepared the way for his masterpiece of deception in the development of spiritualism" (*ibid.* 561).

After what event can we expect a special manifestation of his marvelous workings?

"By the decree enforcing the institution of the papacy in violation of the law of God, our nation will disconnect herself fully from righteousness. When Protestantism shall stretch her hand across the gulf to grasp the hand of the Roman power, when she shall reach over the abyss to clasp hands with spiritualism, when, under the influence of this threefold union, our country shall repudiate every principle of its Constitution as a Protestant and republican government, and shall make provision for the propagation of papal falsehoods and delusions, then we may know that the time has come for the marvelous working of Satan and that the end is near" (5T 451).

Will the evil spirits advocate the keeping of the Sabbath or Sunday?

"The miracle-working power manifested through spiritualism will exert its influence against those who choose to obey God rather than men. Communications from the spirits will declare that God has sent them to convince the rejecters of Sunday of their error, affirming the laws of the land should be obeyed as the law of God" (GC 590, 591).

Through what particular means will Satan deceive many?

"Fearful sights of a supernatural character will soon be revealed in the heavens, in token of the power of miracle-working demons" (*ibid.* 624).

"Persons will arise pretending to be Christ Himself, and claiming the title and worship which belong to the world's Redeemer. They will perform wonderful miracles of healing and will profess to have revelations from heaven contradicting the testimony of the Scriptures" *(ibid.)*.

"The sick will be healed before us. Miracles will be performed in our sight. Are we prepared for the trial which awaits us when the lying wonders of Satan shall be more fully exhibited?" (1T 302).

"Satan can, through a species of deceptions, perform wonders that will appear to be genuine miracles. It was this he hoped to make a test question with the Israelites at the time of their deliverance from Egypt" (2SM 52).

Does he really heal the sick?

"Wonderful scenes, with which Satan will be closely connected, will soon take place. God's Word declares that Satan will work miracles. He will make people sick, and then will suddenly remove from them his satanic power. They will then be regarded as healed. These works of apparent healing will bring Seventh-day Adventists to the test" *(ibid.* 53).

"Men under the influence of evil spirits will work miracles. They will make people sick by casting their spell upon them, and will then remove the spell, leading others to say that those who were sick have been miraculously healed. This Satan has done again and again" *(ibid.)*.

"He will take possession of human bodies, and make men and women sick. Then he will suddenly cease to exercise his evil power, and it will be proclaimed that a miracle has been wrought" (MM 110).

Can we expect a cessation of these lying wonders once they have begun?

"We are warned that in the last days he will work with signs and lying wonders. And he will continue these wonders until the close of probation, that he may point to them as evidence that he is an angel of light and not of darkness" (2SM 51 [7BC 911; 5BC 1099]).

What Elijah-type miracle will be performed by some of Satan's devoted followers?

"It is stated in the Word that the enemy will work through his agents who have departed from the faith, and they will seemingly work miracles, even to the bringing down of fire out of heaven in the sight of men" (2SM 54).

"We must not trust the claims of men. They may, as Christ represents, profess to work miracles in healing the sick. Is this marvelous, when just behind them stands the great deceiver, the miracle worker who will yet bring down fire from heaven in the sight of men?" (*ibid.* 49).

"I saw that soon it would be considered blasphemy to speak against the rapping, and that it would spread more and more, that Satan's power would increase and some of his devoted followers would have power to work miracles and even to bring down fire from heaven in the sight of men" (EW 59 [EW 86, 87]).

"Servants of God, with their faces lighted up and shining with holy consecration, will hasten from place to place to proclaim the message from heaven. By thousands of voices, all over the earth, the warning will be given.

Miracles will be wrought, the sick will be healed, and signs and wonders will follow the believers. Satan also works with lying wonders, even bringing down fire from heaven in the sight of men (Rev. 13:13). Thus the inhabitants of the earth will be brought to take their stand" (GC 612).

"It is the lying wonders of the devil that will take the world captive, and he will cause fire to come down from heaven in the sight of men. He is to work miracles; and this wonderful, miracle-working power is to sweep in the whole world" (2SM 51).

"He claims to be Christ, and he is coming in, pretending to be the great medical missionary. He will cause fire to come down from heaven in the sight of men, to prove that he is God" (MM 87, 88).

Is this real fire, or does it just have the appearance of fire?

"'He doeth great wonders, so that he maketh fire come down from heaven on the earth in the sight of men, and deceiveth them that dwell on the earth by the means of those miracles which he had power to do' (Rev. 13:13, 14). No mere impostures are here foretold. Men are deceived by the miracles which Satan's agents have power to do, not which they pretend to do" (GC 553).

How will the enemies of Christ look upon the ability to perform miracles?

"Papists, who boast of miracles as a certain sign of the true church, will be readily deceived by this wonder-working power" (*ibid.* 588).

"When the enemies of Christ, by the instigation of Satan, request them to show some miracle, they should answer them as meekly as the Son of God answered Satan, 'It is written, Thou shalt not tempt the Lord thy God.' If they will not be convinced by inspired testimony, a manifestation of God's power would not benefit them" (4aSG 150).

"Unbelievers will require them to do some miracle, if they believe God's special power is in the church, and that they are the chosen people of God. Unbelievers, who are afflicted with infirmities, will require them to work a miracle upon them, if God is with them. Christ's followers should imitate the example of their Lord. Jesus, with His divine power, did not do any mighty works for Satan's diversion. Neither can the servants of Christ. They should refer the unbelieving to the written, inspired testimony for evidence of their being the loyal people of God, and heirs of salvation" (*ibid.* 151).

Who will the multitude think is working so marvelously in their churches?

"Before the final visitation of God's judgments upon the earth there will be among the people of the Lord such a revival of primitive godliness as has not been witnessed since apostolic times. . . . The enemy of souls desires to hinder this work; and before the time for such a movement shall come, he will endeavor to prevent it by introducing a counterfeit. In those churches which he can bring under his deceptive power he will make it appear that God's special blessing is poured out; there will be manifest what is thought to be great religious interest. Multitudes will exult that God is working marvelously for them, when the work is that of another spirit. Under a religious guise, Satan will seek to extend his influence over the Christian world" (GC 464).

"Before the loud cry of the third angel is given, he [Satan] raises an excitement in these religious bodies, that those who have rejected the truth may think that God is with them. He hopes to deceive the honest and lead them to think that God is still working for the churches. But the light will shine, and all who are honest will leave the fallen churches, and take their stand with the remnant" (EW 261).

"Through the agency of spiritualism, miracles will be wrought . . . and many undeniable wonders will be performed. And as the spirits will profess faith in the Bible, and manifest respect for the institutions of the church, their work will be accepted as a manifestation of divine power" (GC 588).

Will miracles also accompany the ministry of God's people during the "loud cry"?

"In visions of the night, representations passed before me of a great reformatory movement among God's people. Many were praising God. The sick were healed, and other miracles were wrought. A spirit of intercession was seen, even as was manifested before the great day of Pentecost. Hundreds and thousands were seen visiting families, and opening before them the Word of God. Hearts were convicted by the power of the Holy Spirit, and a spirit of genuine conversion was manifest. On every side doors were thrown open to the proclamation of the truth. The world seemed to be lightened with the heavenly influence. Great blessings were received by the true and humble people of God" (9T 126).

How should we regard miracles? Will they be a test as they were in Elijah's day?

"The way in which Christ worked was to preach the Word, and to relieve suffering by miraculous works of healing. But I am instructed that we cannot now work in this way, for Satan will exercise his power by working miracles. God's servants today could not work by means of miracles, because spurious works of healing, claiming to be divine, will be wrought" (2SM 54).

"If we accept not the truth in the love of it, we may be among the number who will see the miracles wrought by Satan in these last days, and believe them. Many strange things will appear as wonderful miracles, which should be regarded as deceptions manufactured by the father of lies" (*ibid.* 53).

"Satan, surrounded by evil angels, and claiming to be God, will work miracles of all kinds, to deceive, if possible, the very elect. God's people will not find their safety in working miracles, for Satan will counterfeit the miracles that will be wrought" (9T 16 [see also 2SM 55]).

How can we tell the true from the false?

"If those through whom cures are performed are disposed, on account of these manifestations, to excuse their neglect of the law of God, and continue in disobedience, though they have power to any and every extent, it does not follow that they have the great power of God. On the contrary, it is the miracle-working power of the great deceiver" (5BC 1099).

"The last great delusion is soon to open before us. Antichrist is to perform his marvelous works in our sight. So closely will the counterfeit resemble the true that it will be impossible to distinguish between them except by the Holy Scriptures. By their testimony every statement and every miracle must be tested" (GC 593).

"The Bible will never be superseded by miraculous manifestations" (2SM 48).

What is Satan's most successful and fascinating delusion?

"Satan is finding access to thousands of minds by presenting himself under the guise of departed friends. . . .

Through spiritualism many of the sick, the bereaved, the curious, are communicating with evil spirits. All who venture to do this are on dangerous ground" (RH Sept. 7, 1911).

"It is Satan's most successful and fascinating delusion, one calculated to take hold of the sympathies of those who have laid their loved ones in the grave. Evil angels come in the form of those loved ones, and relate incidents connected with their lives, and perform acts which they performed while living. In this way they lead persons to believe that their dead friends are angels, hovering over them, and communicating with them. These evil angels, who assume to be the deceased friends, are regarded with a certain idolatry, and with many their word has greater weight than the Word of God" (ST Aug. 26, 1889).

How real does the counterfeit appear to be?

"He has power to bring before men the appearance of their departed friends. The counterfeit is perfect; the familiar look, the words, the tone, are reproduced with marvelous distinctness" (GC 552).

"Their loved ones will appear in robes of light, as familiar to the sight as when they were upon the earth" (RH Apr. 1, 1875).

Will this be an isolated experience, or will many people be confronted by evil angels personating their dead loved ones?

"Many will be confronted by the spirits of devils personating beloved relatives or friends and declaring the most dangerous heresies. These visitants will appeal to our tenderest sympathies and will work miracles to sustain their pretensions" (GC 560).

"It is not difficult for the evil angels to represent both saints and sinners who have died, and make these representations visible to human eyes. These manifestations will be more frequent, and developments of a more startling character will appear as we near the close of time" (Ev 604).

"I saw that the saints must get a thorough understanding of present truth, which they will be obliged to maintain from the Scriptures. They must understand the state of the dead; for the spirits of devils will yet appear to them, professing to be beloved friends and relatives, who will declare to them that the Sabbath has been changed, also other unscriptural doctrines. They will do all in their power to excite sympathy and will work miracles before them to confirm what they declare" (EW 87).

Who else will the lying spirits personate?

"The apostles, as personated by these lying spirits, are made to contradict what they wrote at the dictation of the Holy Spirit when on earth. They deny the divine origin of the Bible" (GC 557).

"The enemy is preparing to deceive the whole world by his miracle-working power. He will assume to personate the angels of light, to personate Jesus Christ" (2SM 21 [2SM 96]).

SATAN'S PERSONATION OF CHRIST

What is Satan's masterpiece of deception? Who does he make himself out to be?

"The conflict is to wax fiercer and fiercer. Satan will take the field and personate Christ. He will misrepresent, misapply, and pervert everything he possibly can, to deceive, if possible, the very elect" (TM 411).

"A power from beneath is working to bring about the last great scenes in the drama—Satan coming as Christ, and working with all deceivableness of unrighteousness in those who are binding themselves together in secret societies" (8T 28 [6BC 1106]).

"If men are so easily misled now, how will they stand when Satan shall personate Christ, and work miracles? Who will be unmoved by his misrepresentations then—professing to be Christ when it is only Satan assuming the person of Christ, and apparently working the works of Christ? What will hold God's people from giving their allegiance to false christs? 'Go not after them' (Luke 17:23)" (2SM 394, 395 [see also 2SM 58]).

How close is Satan's resemblance to Christ?

"It was by the display of supernatural power, in making the serpent his medium, that Satan caused the fall of Adam and Eve in Eden. Before the close of time he will work still greater wonders. So far as his power extends, he will perform actual miracles. . . . But there is a limit beyond which Satan cannot go; and here he calls deception to his aid and counterfeits the work which he has not power actually to perform. In the last days he will appear in such a manner as to make men believe him to be Christ come the second time into the world. He will indeed transform himself into an angel of light. But while he will bear the appearance of Christ in every particular, so far as mere appearance goes, it will deceive none but those who, like Pharaoh, are seeking to resist the truth" (5T 698).

"Satan will work with all deceivableness of unrighteousness to personate Jesus Christ; if it were possible, he would deceive the very elect. Now if the counterfeit bears so close a resemblance to the genuine, is it not essential to be on your guard, that no man deceive you?" (2SM 87).

"Satan is not permitted to counterfeit the manner of Christ's advent" (GC 625).

What will Satan do and say and how will the people respond?

"As the crowning act in the great drama of deception, Satan himself will personate Christ. The church has long professed to look to the Saviour's advent as the consummation of her hopes. Now the great deceiver will make it appear that Christ has come. In different parts of the earth, Satan will manifest himself among men as a majestic being of dazzling brightness, resembling the description of the Son of God given by John in the Revelation (Rev. 1:13-15). The glory that surrounds him is unsurpassed by anything that mortal eyes have yet beheld. The shout of triumph rings out upon the air: 'Christ has come! Christ has come!' The people prostrate themselves in adoration before him, while he lifts up his hands and pronounces a blessing upon them, as Christ blessed His disciples when He was upon the earth. His voice is soft and subdued, yet full of melody. In gentle, compassionate tones he presents some of the same gracious, heavenly truths which the Saviour uttered; he heals the diseases of the people, and then, in his assumed character of Christ, he claims to have changed the Sabbath to Sunday, and commands all to hallow the day which he has blessed. He declares that those who persist in keeping holy the seventh day are blaspheming his name by refusing to listen to his angels sent to them with light and truth. This is the strong, almost overmastering delusion. Like the Samaritans who were deceived by Simon Magus, the multitudes, from the least to the greatest, give heed to these sorceries, saying: This is 'the great power of God'" (*ibid.* 624, 625).

"As the second appearing of our Lord Jesus Christ draws near, satanic agencies are moved from beneath. Satan will not only appear as a human being, but he will personate Jesus Christ; and the world that has rejected the truth will receive him as the Lord of lords and King of kings" (5BC 1105, 1106).

Will he even be accepted by heads of government?

"Disguised as an angel of light, he will walk the earth as a wonder-worker. In beautiful language he will present lofty sentiments. Good words will be spoken by him, and good deeds performed. Christ will be personified, but on one point there will be a marked distinction. Satan will turn the people from the law of God. Notwithstanding this, so well will he counterfeit righteousness, that if it were possible, he would deceive the very elect. Crowned heads, presidents, rulers in high places, will bow to his false theories" (FE 471, 472).

What shall we do when we are commanded to worship him?

"Satan came as an angel of light in the wilderness of

temptation to deceive Christ; and he does not come to man in a hideous form, as he is sometimes represented, but as an angel of light. He will come personating Jesus Christ, working mighty miracles; and men will fall down and worship him as Jesus Christ. We shall be commanded to worship this being, whom the world will glorify as Christ. What shall we do? Tell them that Christ has warned us against just such a foe, who is man's worst enemy, yet who claims to be God; and that when Christ shall make His appearance, it will be with power and great glory, accompanied by ten thousand times ten thousand angels and thousands of thousands; and that when He shall come, we shall know His voice" (6BC 1105, 1106 [RH Dec. 18, 1888]).

To what pinnacle will the apostate churches eventually exalt Satan?

"In this age antichrist will appear as the true Christ, and then the law of God will be fully made void in the nations of our world. Rebellion against God's holy law will be fully ripe. But the true leader of all this rebellion is Satan clothed as an angel of light. Men will be deceived and will exalt him to the place of God, and deify him. But Omnipotence will interpose, and to the apostate churches that unite in the exaltation of Satan, the sentence will go forth, 'Therefore shall her plagues come in one day, death, and mourning, and famine; and she shall be utterly burned with fire: for strong is the Lord God who judgeth her'" (TM 62).

When does the outpouring of the wrath of God (seven last plagues) occur in relationship to Satan's personation of Christ?

"Little by little he has prepared the way for his masterpiece of deception in the development of spiritualism. He has not yet reached the full accomplishment of his designs;

but it will be reached in the last remnant of time. Says the prophet: 'I saw three unclean spirits like frogs; . . . they are the spirits of devils, working miracles, which go forth unto the kings of the earth and of the whole world, to gather them to the battle of that great day of God Almighty' (Rev. 16:13, 14). Except those who are kept by the power of God, through faith in His Word, the whole World will be swept into the ranks of this delusion. The people are fast being lulled to a fatal security, to be awakened only by the outpouring of the wrath of God" (GC 561, 562).

"After putting Jesus in the background, they attract the attention of the world to themselves and to their miracles and lying wonders, which, they declare, far exceed the works of Christ. Thus the world is taken in the snare and lulled to a feeling of security, not to find out their awful deception until the seven last plagues shall be poured out" (EW 266).

"But the people of God will not be misled. The teachings of this false christ are not in accordance with the Scriptures. His blessing is pronounced upon the worshipers of the beast and his image, the very class upon whom the Bible declares that God's unmingled wrath shall be poured out" (GC 625).

How long will Satan remain on the earth in his Christlike form?

There is no information on this point. He apparently will not be visible at the time of the seventh plague or the people would angrily turn against him, "But all unite in heaping their bitterest condemnation upon the ministers" (*ibid.* 655).

How should we prepare for Satan's deceptions so that we shall be able to withstand his wonderful miracle-working power?

"Go to God for yourselves, pray for divine enlightenment, that you may know that you do know what is truth, that when the wonderful miracle-working power of Satan shall be displayed, and the enemy shall come as an angel of light, you may distinguish between the genuine work of God and the imitative work of the powers of darkness" (RH Extra Dec. 24, 1889).

"Many who embraced the third message had not had an experience in the two former messages. Satan understood this, and his evil eye was upon them to overthrow them; but the third angel was pointing them to the most holy place, and those who had had an experience in the past messages were pointing them the way to the heavenly sanctuary. Many saw the perfect chain of truth in the angels' messages, and gladly received them in their order, and followed Jesus by faith into the heavenly sanctuary. These messages were represented to me as an anchor to the people of God. Those who understand and receive them will be kept from being swept away by the many delusions of Satan" (EW 256).

Do all Seventh-day Adventists agree that Satan will personate Christ prior to the close of probation?

No, they do not. Many able students of the Bible and the Spirit of Prophecy locate Satan's personation of Christ at the time of the sixth plague. The two principal E. G. White quotations given in support of this view are:

"Little by little he has prepared the way for his masterpiece of deception in the development of spiritualism. He has not yet reached the full accomplishment of his designs; but it will be reached in the last remnant of time. Says the prophet: 'I saw three unclean spirits like frogs; . . . they are the spirits of devils, working miracles, which go forth unto the kings of the earth and of the whole world, to gather them to the battle of that great day of God Almighty' (Rev.

16:13, 14). Except those who are kept by the power of God, through faith in His Word, the whole world will be swept into the ranks of this delusion" (GC 561, 562).

"Fearful sights of a supernatural character will soon be revealed in the heavens, in token of the power of miracle-working demons. The spirits of devils will go forth to the kings of the earth and of the whole world, to fasten them in deception, and urge them on to unite with Satan in his last struggle against the government of heaven. By these agencies, rulers and subjects will be alike deceived. Persons will arise pretending to be Christ Himself, and claiming the title and worship which belong to the world's Redeemer. They will perform wonderful miracles of healing and will profess to have revelations from heaven contradicting the testimony of the Scriptures.

"As the crowning act in the great drama of deception, Satan himself will personate Christ" (*ibid.* 624).

Sister White's use of the phrase "the last remnant of time" and her use of sixth plague language in describing Satan's dramatic appearance as Christ are considered to be compelling arguments in favor of locating this deception at the time of the sixth plague.

This line of reasoning is not necessarily conclusive, however. The phrase "the last remnant of time" does not point to the future alone. Sister White says that we are in this time now: "Satan as a powerful general has taken the field, and in this last remnant of time he is working through all conceivable methods to close the door against light that God would have come to His people" (RH Extra Dec. 24, 1889). "We are living in the last remnant of time" (Ev 217 [1903]).

Furthermore, her use of sixth-plague language is not limited to some future period. It is true that the devils go forth to the whole world at the time of the sixth plague, but this is exactly what Satan is doing today. "The Spirit of God is gradually withdrawing from the world. Satan is also mustering his forces of evil, going forth 'unto the kings of the earth and of the whole world,' to gather them under his banner, to be trained for 'the battle of that great day of God Almighty'" (7BC 983 [1890]).

In the light of these last two E. G. White quotations we may conclude that it is perfectly reasonable to apply the phrases "the last remnant of time" and Satan's going forth "unto the kings of the earth" to some point before probation's close. Hence his masterpiece of deception, the personation of Christ, may also be located before probation's close.

THE HOLY SPIRIT

What was Christ's favorite subject?

"Christ, the Great Teacher, had an infinite variety of subjects from which to choose, but the one upon which He dwelt most largely was the endowment of the Holy Spirit" (1SM 156).

In God's plan for our redemption, how important is the gift of His Spirit?

"In the gift of the Spirit, Jesus gave to man the highest good that heaven could bestow" (OHC 150).

"Before offering Himself as the sacrificial victim, Christ sought for the most essential and complete gift to bestow upon His followers, a gift that would bring within their reach the boundless resources of grace. 'I will pray the Father,' He said, 'and He shall give you another Comforter'" (DA 668, 669).

"The Holy Spirit was the highest of all gifts that He could solicit from His Father for the exaltation of His people. The Spirit was to be given as a regenerating agent, and without this the sacrifice of Christ would have been of no avail" (*ibid.* 671).

"Only to those who wait humbly upon God, who watch for His guidance and grace, is the Spirit given. The power of God awaits their demand and reception. This promised blessing, claimed by faith, brings all other blessings in its train" (*ibid.* 672).

Do we appreciate this promised Gift as we should?

"Just prior to His leaving His disciples for the heavenly

courts, Jesus encouraged them with the promise of the Holy Spirit. This promise belongs as much to us as it did to them, and yet how rarely it is presented before the people, and its reception spoken of in the church. In consequence of this silence upon this most important theme, what promise do we know less about by its practical fulfillment than this rich promise of the gift of the Holy Spirit, whereby efficiency is to be given to all our spiritual labor? The promise of the Holy Spirit is casually brought into our discourses, is incidentally touched upon, and that is all. Prophecies have been dwelt upon, doctrines have been expounded; but that which is essential to the church in order that they may grow in spiritual strength and efficiency, in order that the preaching may carry conviction with it, and souls be converted to God, has been largely left out of ministerial effort" (TM 174 [see also 8T 21]).

Do we have to put away all of our sins before we receive the Holy Spirit, or does the Holy Spirit help us to put away our sins?

John 16:7-9.

"Without the divine working, man could do no good thing. God calls every man to repentance, yet man cannot even repent unless the Holy Spirit works upon his heart" (8T 64).

"It is the Spirit that convinces of sin, and, with the consent of the human being, expels sin from the heart" (OHC 152).

"The Lord Jesus acts through the Holy Spirit, for it is His representative. Through it He infuses spiritual life into the soul, quickening its energies for good, cleansing from moral defilement, and giving it a fitness for His kingdom" (*ibid.* 152).

How does the miracle of the new birth take place?

John 3:5; 1 Cor. 6:11.

"There is a death to self and sin, and a new life altogether. This change can be brought about only by the effectual working of the Holy Spirit" (DA 172).

"The work of the Holy Spirit upon the heart" "can no more be explained than can the movements of the wind. A person may not be able to tell the exact time or place, or to trace all the circumstances in the process of conversion; but this does not prove him to be unconverted. By an agency as unseen as the wind, Christ is constantly working upon the heart. Little by little, perhaps unconsciously to the receiver, impressions are made that tend to draw the soul to Christ. These may be received through meditating upon Him, through reading the Scriptures, or through hearing the Word from the living preacher. Suddenly, as the Spirit comes with more direct appeal, the soul gladly surrenders itself to Jesus. By many this is called sudden conversion; but it is the result of long wooing by the Spirit of God, a patient, protracted process" (*ibid.* 172).

"When the Spirit of God takes possession of the heart, it transforms the life. . . . The blessing comes when by faith the soul surrenders itself to God. Then that power which no human eye can see creates a new being in the image of God" (*ibid.* 173).

"It is through the Spirit that Christ dwells in us; and the Spirit of God, received into the heart by faith, is the beginning of the life eternal" (*ibid.* 388).

How often do we need to be converted by the Holy Spirit?

"To follow Jesus requires whole-hearted conversion at the start, and a repetition of this conversion every day" (SD 207).

How only can we, as Christians, resist the many temptations that confront us daily?

Rom. 8:1, 4, 9, 13, 14.

"Sin could be resisted and overcome only through the mighty agency of the Third Person of the Godhead" (DA 671).

"He came to destroy the works of the devil, and He has made provision that the Holy Spirit shall be imparted to every repentant soul, to keep him from sinning" (*ibid.* 311).

"Christ has given His Spirit as a divine power to overcome all hereditary and cultivated tendencies to evil, and to impress His own character upon His church" (*ibid.* 671).

Who actually dwells with us through the presence of the Spirit?

"Through the Spirit, Christ was to abide continually in the hearts of His children. Their union with Him was closer than when He was personally with them" (SC 75).

"The Holy Spirit is the Comforter, as the personal presence of Christ to the soul" (RH Nov. 29, 1892).

"On the day of Pentecost the promised Comforter descended and the power from on high was given and the souls of the believers thrilled with the conscious presence of their ascended Lord" (GC 351).

As the Holy Spirit makes the presence of Jesus real to us, how will this affect our characters?

2 Cor. 3:18; Gal. 5:22, 23; 1 Peter 1:2; 2 Thess. 2:13.

"The impartation of the Spirit is the impartation of the life of Christ. It imbues the receiver with the attributes of Christ" (DA 805).

"Never will the human heart know happiness until it is submitted to be molded by the Spirit of God. The Spirit conforms the renewed soul to the model, Jesus Christ.

Through its influence, enmity against God is changed into faith and love, and pride into humility. The soul perceives the beauty of truth, and Christ is honored in excellence and perfection of character" (OHC 152).

"The Spirit was to glorify Christ by revealing to the world the riches of His grace. The very image of God is to be reproduced in humanity. The honor of God, the honor of Christ, is involved in the perfection of the character of His people" (*ibid.* 154).

"Through faith the Holy Spirit works in the heart to create holiness therein; but this cannot be done unless the human agent will work with Christ. We can be fitted for heaven only through the work of the Holy Spirit upon the heart. . . . It is the work of the Holy Spirit to elevate the taste, to sanctify the heart, to ennoble the whole man" (RH Nov. 1, 1892).

THE LATTER RAIN

Has there ever been a time since the entrance of sin that God has not worked by His Holy Spirit?

Gen. 6:3; Isa. 63:10, 11.

"From the beginning, God has been working by His Holy Spirit" (AA 53).

"It is the work of the Holy Spirit from age to age to impart love to human hearts, for love is the living principle of brotherhood" (8T 139).

"During the patriarchal age the influence of the Holy Spirit had often been revealed in a marked manner, but never in its fullness" (AA 37).

What operation of nature does the Lord use to illustrate the work of the Holy Spirit?

Zech. 10:1; Hosea 6:3; Joel 2:28.

"'He will cause to come down for you the rain, the former rain, and the latter rain.' . . . The Lord employs these operations of nature to represent the work of the Holy Spirit" (TM 506).

What is the function of the early rain (which, in Palestine, comes late in October or in November)?

"In the East the former rain falls at the sowingtime. It is necessary in order that the seed may germinate. Under the influence of the fertilizing showers, the tender shoot springs up" *(ibid.).*

What is the function of the latter rain (in March or early April)?

"The latter rain, falling near the close of the season, ripens the grain and prepares it for the sickle" *(ibid.)*.

How does the early rain represent the work of the Holy Spirit in the individual heart?

"As the dew and the rain are given first to cause the seed to germinate, and then to ripen the harvest, so the Holy Spirit is given to carry forward, from one stage to another, the process of spiritual growth" *(ibid.)*.

"At no point in our experience can we dispense with the assistance of that which enables us to make the first start. The blessings received under the former rain are needful to us to the end" *(ibid.* 507).

How does the latter rain represent the Holy Spirit's work with individuals?

"The ripening of the grain represents the completion of the work of God's grace in the soul. By the power of the Holy Spirit the moral image of God is to be perfected in the character. We are to be wholly transformed into the likeness of Christ" *(ibid.* 506).

"The Holy Spirit seeks to abide in each soul. If He is welcomed as an honored guest, those who receive Him will be made complete in Christ. The good work begun will be finished; the holy thoughts, heavenly affections, and Christlike actions will take the place of impure thoughts, perverse sentiments, and rebellious acts" (CH 561).

"As we seek God for the Holy Spirit, it will work in us meekness, humbleness of mind, a conscious dependence upon God for the perfecting latter rain" (TM 509).

What are some of the occasions the Lord sends His Spirit to His people?

"The convocations of the church, as in camp meetings, the assemblies of the home church, and all occasions where there is personal labor for souls, are God's appointed opportunities for giving the early and the latter rain" (*ibid.* 508).

Can isolated individuals have the latter rain of the Holy Spirit in their own lives even though most of their neighbors may not be receiving this blessing?

Gen. 5:24.

"The godly character of this prophet [Enoch] represents the state of holiness which must be attained by those who shall be 'redeemed from the earth' (Rev. 14:3) at the time of Christ's second advent" (PP 88, 89).

"And there are Enochs in this our day" (COL 332).

How does the early rain represent the work of the Spirit for the entire Christian church as a whole?

"The outpouring of the Spirit in the days of the apostles was the beginning of the early, or former, rain, and glorious was the result. To the end of time the presence of the Spirit is to abide with the true church" (AA 54, 55).

"Evil had been accumulating for centuries, and could only be restrained and resisted by the mighty power of the Holy Spirit, the Third Person of the Godhead, who would come with no modified energy, but in the fullness of divine power" (TM 392).

What preparation in heart and life had the disciples made that made the early rain on the church possible?

"They did not wait in idleness. The record says that

they were 'continually in the temple, praising and blessing God' (Luke 24:53)" (AA 35).

"They humbled their hearts in true repentance and confessed their unbelief" (*ibid.* 36).

"The disciples prayed with intense earnestness for a fitness to meet men and in their daily intercourse to speak words that would lead sinners to Christ" (*ibid.* 37).

"Putting away all differences, all desire for the supremacy, they came close together in Christian fellowship" *(ibid.)*.

"It was after the disciples had come into perfect unity, when they were no longer striving for the highest place, that the Spirit was poured out" (8T 20).

"They were weighted with the burden of the salvation of souls" (AA 37).

How did the early rain affect the spirituality of the church members?

"Under the influence of the Spirit, words of penitence and confession mingled with songs of praise for sins forgiven" (*ibid.* 38).

"Those who at Pentecost were endued with power from on high were not thereby freed from further temptation and trial. . . . They were compelled to strive with all their God-given powers to reach the measure of the stature of men and women in Christ Jesus" (*ibid.* 49).

"Daily they prayed for fresh supplies of grace, that they might reach higher and still higher toward perfection" (*ibid.* 49).

"Under the Holy Spirit's working even the weakest, by exercising faith in God, learned to improve their entrusted powers and to become sanctified, refined, and ennobled. As in humility they submitted to the molding influence of the Holy Spirit, they received of the fullness of the

Godhead, and were fashioned in the likeness of the divine" (*ibid.* 49, 50).

How did the early rain affect their power for witnessing to others?

"What followed? The sword of the Spirit, newly edged with power and bathed in the lightnings of heaven, cut its way through unbelief. Thousands were converted in a day" (*ibid.* 38).

"The Holy Spirit" "enabled them to speak with fluency languages with which they had heretofore been unacquainted" (*ibid.* 39).

"Their hearts were surcharged with benevolence so full, so deep, so far-reaching, that it impelled them to go to the ends of the earth, testifying to the power of Christ" (*ibid.* 46).

"The appearance of fire signified the fervent zeal with which the apostles would labor and the power that would attend their work" (*ibid.* 39).

"What was the result of the outpouring of the Spirit on the Day of Pentecost? The glad tidings of a risen Saviour were carried to the uttermost parts of the inhabited world" (*ibid.* 48).

"The church beheld converts flocking to her from all directions. Backsliders were reconverted" *(ibid.).*

"The ambition of the believers was to reveal the likeness of Christ's character and to labor for the enlargement of His kingdom" *(ibid.).*

Did the Lord withdraw His Holy Spirit after Pentecost?

"The Lord did not lock the reservoir of heaven after pouring His Spirit upon the early disciples. . . . If we do not have His power, it is because of our spiritual lethargy, our indifference, our indolence. Let us come out of this formality and deadness" (6BC 1055).

How does the latter rain represent the work of the Holy Spirit for the entire Christian church as a whole?

"In the time of the end, when God's work in the earth is closing, the earnest efforts put forth by consecrated believers under the guidance of the Holy Spirit are to be accompanied by special tokens of divine favor" (AA 54).

"The great work of the gospel is not to close with less manifestation of the power of God than marked its opening. The prophecies which were fulfilled in the outpouring of the former rain at the opening of the gospel are again to be fulfilled in the latter rain at its close. Here are the 'times of refreshing' to which the apostle Peter looked forward when he said: 'Repent ye therefore, and be converted, that your sins may be blotted out, when the times of refreshing shall come from the presence of the Lord; and he shall send Jesus (Acts 3:19)'" (GC 611, 612).

"The outpouring of the Spirit in the days of the apostles was 'the former rain,' and glorious was the result. But the latter rain will be more abundant" (8T 21).

"What the Lord did for His people in that time, it is just as essential, and more so, that He do for His people today. All that the apostles did, every church member today is to do. And we are to work with as much more fervor, to be accompanied by the Holy Spirit in as much greater measure, as the increase of wickedness demands a more decided call to repentance" (7T 33).

How will the latter rain affect the spirituality and character development of the church members?

"The latter rain, ripening earth's harvest, represents the spiritual grace that prepares the church for the coming of the Son of man. But unless the former rain has fallen, there will be no life; the green blade will not spring up. Unless the early showers have done their work, the latter rain can bring no seed to perfection" (TM 506).

"Near the close of earth's harvest, a special bestowal of spiritual grace is promised to prepare the church for the coming of the Son of man. This outpouring of the Spirit is likened to the falling of the latter rain" (AA 55).

"It is the latter rain which revives and strengthens them to pass through the time of trouble" (1T 353).

"They have received 'the latter rain,' 'the refreshing from the presence of the Lord,' and they are prepared for the trying hour before them" (GC 613).

"Before the final visitation of God's judgments upon the earth there will be among the people of the Lord such a revival of primitive godliness as has not been witnessed since apostolic times. The Spirit and power of God will be poured out upon His children" (GC 464).

How will the latter rain affect the church's power for witnessing?

"Under the showers of the latter rain the inventions of man, the human machinery, will at times be swept away, the boundary of man's authority will be as broken reeds, and the Holy Spirit will speak through the living, human agent, with convincing power. No one then will watch to see if the sentences are well rounded off, if the grammar is faultless. The living water will flow in God's own channels" (2SM 58, 59).

"They will declare the truth with the might of the Spirit's power. Multitudes will receive the faith and join the armies of the Lord" (Ev 700).

"During the loud cry, the church, aided by the providential interpositions of her exalted Lord, will diffuse the knowledge of salvation so abundantly that light will be communicated to every city and town. The earth will be filled with the knowledge of salvation" (*ibid.* 694).

"Servants of God, with their faces lighted up and shining with holy consecration, will hasten from place to place to proclaim the message from heaven. By thousands of voices, all over the earth, the warning will be given. Miracles will be wrought, the sick will be healed, and signs and wonders will follow the believers" (GC 612).

Will the latter rain come after God's people have been sealed or before the sealing is finished?

"Before the work is closed up and the sealing of God's people is finished, we shall receive the outpouring of the Spirit of God" (1SM 111).

Will the latter rain come before or after the close of probation?

" 'The commencement of the time of trouble,' here mentioned, does not refer to the time when the plagues shall begin to be poured out, but to a short period just before they are poured out, while Christ is in the sanctuary. At that time, while the work of salvation is closing, trouble will be coming on the earth, and the nations will be angry, yet held in check so as not to prevent the work of the third angel. At that time the 'latter rain,' or refreshing from the presence of the Lord, will come, to give power to the loud voice of the third angel, and prepare the saints to stand in the period when the seven last plagues shall be poured out" (EW 85, 86).

Will all of our church members receive the power of the Holy Spirit?

"Are we hoping to see the whole church revived? That time will never come. There are persons in the church who are not converted, and who will not unite in earnest, prevailing prayer. We must enter upon the work individually. We must pray more, and talk less" (1SM 122).

"Those who make no decided effort, but simply wait

for the Holy Spirit to compel them to action, will perish in darkness. You are not to sit still and do nothing in the work of God" (ChS 228).

"Only those who are living up to the light they have will receive greater light. Unless we are daily advancing in the exemplification of the active Christian virtues, we shall not recognize the manifestations of the Holy Spirit in the latter rain. It may be falling on hearts all around us, but we shall not discern or receive it" (TM 507).

"I saw that many were neglecting the preparation so needful, and were looking to the time of 'refreshing' and the 'latter rain' to fit them to stand in the day of the Lord, and to live in His sight. Oh, how many I saw in the time of trouble without a shelter! They had neglected the needful preparation; therefore they could not receive the refreshing that all must have to fit them to live in the sight of a holy God" (EW 71).

What preparation of heart and life must we make in order to be prepared for the special outpouring of God's Holy Spirit?

Earnest Prayer. "We should pray as earnestly for the descent of the Holy Spirit as the disciples prayed on the day of Pentecost. If they needed it at that time, we need it more today. . . . Without the Spirit's aid, our efforts to present divine truth will be in vain" (RH Aug. 25, 1896).

"A revival of true godliness among us is the greatest and most urgent of all our needs. To seek this should be our first work. There must be earnest effort to obtain the blessing of the Lord, not because God is not willing to bestow His blessing upon us, but because we are unprepared to receive it. Our heavenly Father is more willing to give His Holy Spirit to them that ask Him, than are earthly parents to give good gifts to their children. But it is our work, by confession, humiliation, repentance, and earnest prayer, to fulfill the conditions upon which God has promised to grant us His blessing. A revival need be expected only in answer to prayer" (1SM 121).

"We may have had a measure of the Spirit of God, but by prayer and faith we are continually to seek more of the Spirit. It will never do to cease our efforts. If we do not progress, if we do not place ourselves in an attitude to receive both the former and the latter rain, we shall lose our souls, and the responsibility will lie at our own door" (TM 508).

"The measure of the Holy Spirit we receive will be proportioned to the measure of our desire and the faith exercised for it, and the use we shall make of the light and knowledge that shall be given to us. We shall be entrusted with the Holy Spirit according to our capacity to receive and our ability to impart it to others" (RH May 5, 1896).

Cleanse soul temple of every defilement. "May the Lord help His people to cleanse the soul temple from every defilement, and to maintain such a close connection with Him that they may be partakers of the latter rain when it shall be poured out" (6BC 1055 [RH July 20, 1886]).

"The latter rain will come, and the blessing of God will fill every soul that is purified from every defilement. It is our work today to yield our souls to Christ, that we may be fitted for the time of refreshing from the presence of the Lord—fitted for the baptism of the Holy Spirit" (Ev 702 [1SM 191]).

"I was shown that if God's people make no efforts on their part, but wait for the refreshing to come upon them and remove their wrongs and correct their errors; if they depend upon that to cleanse them from filthiness of the flesh and spirit, and fit them to engage in the loud cry of the third angel, they will be found wanting. The refreshing or power of God comes only on those who have prepared themselves for it by doing the work which God bids them, namely, cleansing themselves from all filthiness of the flesh and spirit, perfecting holiness in the fear of God" (1T 619).

"There is nothing that Satan fears so much as that the people of God shall clear the way by removing every hindrance, so that the Lord can pour out His Spirit upon a languishing church. . . . Every temptation, every opposing influence, whether open or secret, may be successfully resisted, 'not by might, not by power, but by my spirit, saith the Lord of Hosts' (Zech. 4:6)" (1SM 124).

"Those who come up to every point, and stand every test, and overcome, be the price what it may, have heeded the counsel of the True Witness, and they will receive the latter rain, and thus be fitted for translation" (1T 187).

Put away all dissension. "Let Christians put away all dissension and give themselves to God for the saving of the lost. Let them ask in faith for the promised blessing, and it will come. The outpouring of the Spirit in the days of the apostles was 'the former rain,' and glorious was the result. But the latter rain will be more abundant" (8T 21 [see also Ev 698]).

"When we bring our hearts into unity with Christ, and our lives into harmony with His work, the Spirit that fell on the disciples on the day of Pentecost will fall on us" (8T 246).

Victory over every wrong word and action. "I saw that none could share the 'refreshing' unless they obtain the victory over every besetment, over pride, selfishness, love of the world, and over every wrong word and action. We should, therefore, be drawing nearer and nearer to the Lord and be earnestly seeking that preparation necessary to enable us to stand in the battle in the day of the Lord" (EW 71).

Study God's Word. "When we as a people understand what this book [the book of Revelation] means to us, there will be seen among us a great revival" (TM 113).

Become active laborers in Christ's service. "The great outpouring of the Spirit of God, which lightens the whole earth with His glory, will not come until we have an enlightened people, that know by experience what it means to be laborers together with God. When we have entire, wholehearted consecration to the service of Christ, God will recognize the fact by an outpouring of His Spirit without measure; but this will not be while the largest portion of the church are not laborers together with God" (Chs 253 [RH July 21, 1896; see also Ev 699]).

"When the churches become living, working churches, the Holy Spirit will be given in answer to their sincere request. . . . Then the windows of heaven will be open for the showers of the latter rain" (RH Feb. 25, 1890).

"When the reproach of indolence and slothfulness shall have been wiped away from the church, the Spirit of the Lord will be graciously manifested. Divine power will be revealed. The church will see the providential working of the Lord of hosts. The light of truth will shine forth in clear, strong rays, and, as in the time of the apostles, many souls will turn from error to truth. The earth will be lighted with the glory of the Lord" (9T 46).

When we do our part, what will God do?

"When the way is prepared for the Spirit of God, the blessing will come. Satan can no more hinder a shower of blessing from descending upon God's people than he can close the windows of heaven that rain cannot come upon the earth" (1SM 124).

"The answer may come with sudden velocity and overpowering might; or it may be delayed for days and weeks, and our faith receive a trial. But God knows how and when to answer our prayer. It is *our* part of the work to put ourselves in connection with the divine channel. God is responsible for *His* part of the work. He is faithful who hath promised. The great and important matter with us is to be of one heart and mind, putting aside all envy and malice, and, as humble supplicants, to watch and wait. Jesus, our Representative and Head, is ready to do for us what He did for the praying, watching ones on the day of Pentecost" (quoted in *Our Firm Foundation,* Vol. II, p. 683).

THE
LOUD CRY

What is God's last warning message to be given to the world?

Rev. 18:1-5.

"This scripture points forward to a time when the announcement of the fall of Babylon, as made by the second angel of Revelation 14 (verse 8), is to be repeated, with the additional mention of the corruptions which have been entering the various organizations that constitute Babylon, since that message was first given, in the summer of 1844" (GC 603 [see also EW 277]).

"As foretold in the eighteenth of Revelation, the third angel's message is to be proclaimed with great power by those who give the final warning against the beast and his image" (8T 118).

"Revelation 18 points to the time when, as the result of rejecting the threefold warning of Revelation 14:6-12, the church will have fully reached the condition foretold by the second angel, and the people of God still in Babylon will be called upon to separate from her communion. This message is the last that will ever be given to the world" (GC 390).

"These announcements, uniting with the third angel's message, constitute the final warning to be given to the inhabitants of the earth" (*ibid.* 604).

Is this the same message we have been preaching since 1844, or is it a distinct call?

"When Jesus began His public ministry, He cleansed

the Temple from its sacrilegious profanation. Among the last acts of His ministry was the second cleansing of the Temple. So in the last work for the warning of the world, two distinct calls are made to the churches. The second angel's message is 'Babylon is fallen, is fallen, that great city, because she made all nations drink of the wine of the wrath of her fornication' (Rev. 14:8). And in the loud cry of the third angel's message a voice is heard from heaven saying, 'Come out of her, my people, that ye be not partakers of her sins, and that ye receive not of her plagues. For her sins have reached unto heaven, and God hath remembered her iniquities' (Rev. 18:4, 5)" (2SM 118 [7BC 985; see also EW 277]).

What is the very heart of the three angels' messages?

Rev. 14:6.

"Several have written to me, inquiring if the message of justification by faith is the third angel's message, and I have answered, 'It is the third angel's message in verity'" (Ev 190 [1SM 372]).

"The message of Christ's righteousness is to sound from one end of the earth to the other to prepare the way of the Lord. This is the glory of God, which closes the work of the third angel" (6T 19).

"The Lord in His great mercy sent a most precious message to His people through Elders Waggoner and Jones. This message was to bring more prominently before the world the uplifted Saviour, the sacrifice for the sins of the whole world. It presented justification through faith in the Surety; it invited the people to receive the righteousness of Christ, which is made manifest in obedience to all the commandments of God. Many had lost sight of Jesus. They needed to have their eyes directed to His divine person, His merits, and His changeless love for the human family. All power is given into His hands, that He may dispense rich gifts unto men, imparting the priceless gift of His own righteousness to the helpless human agent. This is the message that God commanded to be given to the world. It is the third angel's message, which is to be proclaimed with a loud voice, and attended with the outpouring of His Spirit in a large measure" (TM 91, 92).

"The last message of mercy to be given to the world is a revelation of His character of love. The children of God are to manifest His glory. In their own life and character they are to reveal what the grace of God has done for them" (COL 415, 416).

Why is this message said to be given with a "strong voice" or "loud cry"?

Rev. 18:2.

"It is represented as being given with a loud voice; that is, with the power of the Holy Spirit" (7BC 980).

What makes the loud cry possible? Whence its compelling power?

Zech. 4:6.

"The 'latter rain,' or refreshing from the presence of the Lord, will come, to give power to the loud voice of the third angel, and prepare the saints to stand in the period when the seven last plagues shall be poured out" (EW 86).

"I heard those clothed with the armor speak forth the truth with great power. It had effect. . . . I asked what had made this great change. An angel answered, 'It is the latter rain, the refreshing from the presence of the Lord, the loud cry of the third angel'" (EW 271).

To whom is the loud cry particularly directed?

"In the eighteenth chapter of the Revelation the people

of God are called upon to come out of Babylon. According to this scripture, many of God's people must still be in Babylon. And in what religious bodies are the greater part of the followers of Christ now to be found? Without doubt, in the various churches professing the Protestant faith" (GC 383).

"It is true that there are real Christians in the Roman Catholic communion. Thousands in that church are serving God according to the best light they have. . . . Many will yet take their position with His people" (*ibid.* 565).

"Notwithstanding the spiritual darkness and alienation from God that exist in the churches which constitute Babylon, the great body of Christ's true followers are still to be found in their communion" (*ibid.* 390).

What will Satan introduce into the popular churches before Revelation 18:1 is fulfilled?

"The enemy of souls desires to hinder this work; and before the time for such a movement shall come, he will endeavor to prevent it by introducing a counterfeit. In those churches which he can bring under his deceptive power he will make it appear that God's special blessing is poured out; there will be manifest what is thought to be great religious interest. Multitudes will exult that God is working marvelously for them, when the work is that of another spirit. Under a religious guise, Satan will seek to extend his influence over the Christian world" (*ibid.* 464).

How can we differentiate between Satan's false revival and the loud cry?

"There is an emotional excitement, a mingling of the true with the false, that is well adapted to mislead. Yet none need be deceived. In the light of God's Word it is not difficult to determine the nature of these movements.

Wherever men neglect the testimony of the Bible, turning away from those plain, soul-testing truths which require self-denial and renunciation of the world, there we may be sure that God's blessing is not bestowed. And by the rule which Christ Himself has given, 'Ye shall know them by their fruits' (Matt. 7:16), it is evident that these movements are not the work of the Spirit of God" (GC 464, 465).

Do we know exactly when the latter rain will fall and the angel of Revelation 18 will come down from heaven?

"I have no specific time of which to speak when the outpouring of the Holy Spirit will take place—when the mighty angel will come down from heaven, and unite with the third angel in closing up the work for this world; my message is that our only safety is in being ready for the heavenly refreshing" (7BC 984).

Was the fall of Babylon (Rev. 18:2) complete when Mrs. White wrote *The Great Controversy?*

"Not yet, however, can it be said that 'Babylon is fallen, . . . because she made *all nations* drink of the wine of the wrath of her fornication.' She has not yet made all nations do this" (GC 389).

When will Babylon's fall be complete so that Revelation 18:2 can be preached as a wholly fulfilled prophecy?

" 'She made all nations drink of the wine of the wrath of her fornication' (Rev. 14:8). How is this done? By forcing men to accept a spurious sabbath" (8T 94).

"Not until this condition shall be reached, and the union of the church with the world shall be fully accomplished throughout Christendom, will the fall of Babylon be complete. The change is a progressive one, and the perfect fulfillment of Revelation 14:8 is yet future" (GC 390).

How will Sunday legislation with its accompanying persecution affect the preaching of the third angel's message?

"When the storm of persecution really breaks upon us, the true sheep will hear the true Shepherd's voice. . . . Then will the message of the third angel swell to a loud cry, and the whole earth will be lightened with the glory of the Lord" (6T 401).

"At the commencement of the time of trouble, we were filled with the Holy Ghost as we went forth and proclaimed the Sabbath more fully" (EW 33 [see also EW 85]).

"This false Sabbath is to be enforced by an oppressive law. Satan and his angels are wide awake and intensely active. . . . But while Satan works with his lying wonders, the time will be fulfilled foretold in the Revelation, and the mighty angel that shall lighten the earth with his glory will proclaim the fall of Babylon, and call upon God's people to forsake her" (7BC 985 [RH Dec. 13, 1892]).

How will this wonderful experience affect the people of God?

"As the members of the body of Christ approach the period of their last conflict, 'the time of Jacob's trouble,' they will grow up into Christ, and will partake largely of His Spirit. As the third message swells to a loud cry, and as great power and glory attend the closing work, the faithful people of God will partake of that glory. It is the latter rain which revives and strengthens them to pass through the time of trouble. Their faces will shine with the glory of that light which attends the third angel" (7BC 984 [1T 353]).

"As the third angel's message swells into a loud cry, great power and glory will attend its proclamation. The faces of God's people will shine with the light of heaven" (7T 17).

"As the end approaches, the testimonies of God's servants will become more decided and more powerful" (RH Dec. 13, 1892).

Will it compare in any way with the "midnight cry" of 1844?

"The angel who unites in the proclamation of the third angel's message is to lighten the whole earth with his glory. A work of worldwide extent and unwonted power is here foretold. The advent movement of 1840-44 was a glorious manifestation of the power of God; the first angel's message was carried to every missionary station in the world, and in some countries there was the greatest religious interest which has been witnessed in any land since the Reformation of the sixteenth century; but these are to be exceeded by the mighty movement under the last warning of the third angel" (GC 611).

"I saw that this message will close with power and strength far exceeding the midnight cry" (EW 278).

"The power which stirred the people so mightily in the 1844 movement will again be revealed. The third angel's message will go forth, not in whispered tones, but with a loud voice" (5T 252 [Ev 693]).

What was the "midnight cry" like?

"Like a tidal wave the movement swept over the land. . . . There was little ecstatic joy, but rather deep searching of heart, confession of sin, and forsaking of the world. A preparation to meet the Lord was the burden of agonizing spirits. There was persevering prayer and unreserved consecration to God. . . .

"Of all the great religious movements since the days of the apostles, none have been more free from human imperfection and the wiles of Satan than was that of the autumn of 1844. . . .

"They studied the Word of God with an intensity of interest before unknown. . . . At that time there was faith that brought answers to prayer. . . . The assurance of the Saviour's approval was more necessary to them than their daily food" (GC 400-403).

How will the loud cry compare with Pentecost?

"The work will be similar to that of the Day of Pentecost. As the 'former rain' was given, in the outpouring of the Holy Spirit at the opening of the gospel, to cause the upspringing of the precious seed, so the 'latter rain' will be given at its close for the ripening of the harvest" (*ibid.* 611).

"The outpouring of the Spirit in the days of the apostles was the former rain, and glorious was the result. But the latter rain will be more abundant" (Ev 701).

"The time is coming when there will be as many converted in a day as there were on the day of Pentecost, after the disciples had received the Holy Spirit" (*ibid.* 692).

Will miracles be wrought as at Pentecost and soon thereafter?

"The work will be similar to that of the Day of Pentecost. . . . The great work of the gospel is not to close with less manifestation of the power of God than marked its opening. The prophecies which were fulfilled in the outpouring of the former rain at the opening of the gospel are again to be fulfilled in the latter rain at its close. Here are 'the times of refreshing' to which the apostle Peter looked forward when he said: 'Repent ye therefore, and be converted, that your sins may be blotted out, when the times of refreshing shall come from the presence of the Lord; and he shall send Jesus' (Acts 3:19, 20).

"Servants of God, with their faces lighted up and shining with holy consecration, will hasten from place to place to proclaim the message from heaven. By thousands of voices, all over the earth, the warning will be given. Miracles will be wrought, the sick will be healed, and signs and wonders will follow the believers. Satan also works with lying wonders, even bringing down fire from heaven in the sight of men (Rev. 13:13). Thus the inhabitants of the earth will be brought to take their stand" (GC 611, 612).

"Mighty miracles were wrought, the sick were healed, and signs and wonders followed the believers" (EW 278).

What is God's attitude toward those who deny that He will again work miracles?

"Here we see that the church—the Lord's sanctuary— was the first to feel the stroke of the wrath of God. The ancient men, those to whom God had given great light and who had stood as guardians of the spiritual interests of the people, had betrayed their trust. They had taken the position that we need not look for miracles and the marked manifestation of God's power as in former days" (5T 211).

Is it possible that the gift of tongues may also be repeated?

"It is with an earnest longing that I look forward to the time when the events of the day of Pentecost shall be repeated with even greater power than on that occasion. John says, 'I saw another angel come down from heaven, having great power; and the earth was lightened with his glory.' Then, as at the Pentecostal season, the people will hear the truth spoken to them, every man in his own tongue" (6BC 1055 [RH July 20, 1886]).

How will God's children who are still in Babylon respond to the loud cry?

"Souls that were scattered all through the religious

bodies answered to the call, and the precious were hurried out of the doomed churches, as Lot was hurried out of Sodom before her destruction" (EW 279).

"When the crisis comes, many will be prepared to make right decisions even in the face of the formidable difficulties that will be brought about through the deceptive miracles of Satan. Although these will confess the truth and become workers with Christ at the eleventh hour, they will receive equal wages with those who have wrought through the whole day. There will be an army of steadfast believers who will stand as firm as a rock through the last test" (RH Dec. 24, 1889).

"Why was it that Christ went out by the seaside, and into the mountains? He was to give the word of life to the people. They did not see it just that minute. A good many do not see it now, to take their position, but these things are influencing their lives; and when the message goes with a loud voice, they will be ready for it. They will not hesitate long; they will come out and take their position" (Ev 300, 301).

"The message will be carried not so much by argument as by the deep conviction of the Spirit of God. The arguments have been presented. The seed has been sown, and now it will spring up and bear fruit. The publications distributed by missionary workers have exerted their influence, yet many whose minds were impressed have been prevented from fully comprehending the truth or from yielding obedience. Now the rays of light penetrate everywhere, the truth is seen in its clearness, and the honest children of God sever the bands which have held them. Family connections, church relations, are powerless to stay them now. Truth is more precious than all besides. Notwithstanding the agencies combined against the truth, a large number take their stand upon the Lord's side" (GC 612).

"I heard those clothed with the armor speak forth the truth with great power. It had effect. Many had been bound; some wives by their husbands, and some children by their parents. The honest who had been prevented from hearing the truth now eagerly laid hold upon it. All fear of their relatives was gone, and the truth alone was exalted to them. They had been hungering and thirsting for truth; it was dearer and more precious than life. I asked what had made this great change. An angel answered, 'It is the latter rain, the refreshing from the presence of the Lord, the loud cry of the third angel'" (EW 271).

Will any backslidden Adventists heed the message?

"Many who have strayed from the fold will come back to follow the great Shepherd" (6T 401).

What Spirit of Prophecy book will be instrumental in leading many to take their stand with God's commandment-keeping people?

"The book *The Great Controversy* I appreciate above silver or gold, and I greatly desire that it shall come before the people" (CM 128). "The results of the circulation of *[The Great Controversy]* are not to be judged by what now appears. By reading it, some souls will be aroused, and will have courage to unite themselves at once with those who keep the commandments of God. But a much larger number who read it will not take their position until they see the very events taking place that are foretold in it. The fulfillment of some of the predictions will inspire faith that others also will come to pass, and when the earth is lightened with the glory of the Lord, in the closing work, many souls will take their position on the commandments of God as the result of this agency" (*ibid.* 128, 129).

How will the unconverted members of the Seventh-day Adventist Church react?

"The third angel's message will not be comprehended, the light which will lighten the earth with its glory will be called a false light, by those who refuse to walk in its advancing glory" (RH May 27, 1890).

"Unless those who can help in ―――― are aroused to a sense of their duty, they will not recognize the work of God when the loud cry of the third angel shall be heard" (TM 300).

"There is to be in the churches a wonderful manifestation of the power of God, but it will not move upon those who have not humbled themselves before the Lord, and opened the door of their heart by confession and repentance. In the manifestation of that power which lightens the earth with the glory of God, they will see only something which in their blindness they think dangerous, something which will arouse their fears, and they will brace themselves to resist it. Because the Lord does not work according to their expectations and ideal, they will oppose the work. 'Why,' they say, 'should we not know the Spirit of God, when we have been in the work so many years?'" (RH Nov. 7, 1918).

"As the storm approaches, a large class who have professed faith in the third angel's message, but have not been sanctified through obedience to the truth, abandon their position and join the ranks of the opposition" (GC 608).

What will be the reaction of the popular ministry and the sin-loving multitudes?

"But since many refuse to be satisfied with the mere authority of men and demand a plain 'Thus saith the Lord,' the popular ministry, like the Pharisees of old, filled with anger as their authority is questioned, will denounce the message as of Satan and stir up the sin-loving multitudes to revile and persecute those who proclaim it.

"As the controversy extends into new fields and the minds of the people are called to God's downtrodden law, Satan is astir. The power attending the message will only madden those who oppose it. The clergy will put forth almost superhuman efforts to shut away the light lest it should shine upon their flocks. By every means at their command they will endeavor to suppress the discussion of these vital questions. The church appeals to the strong arm of civil power, and, in this work, papists and Protestants unite. As the movement for Sunday enforcement becomes more bold and decided, the law will be invoked against commandment keepers. They will be threatened with fines and imprisonment, and some will be offered positions of influence, and other rewards and advantages, as inducements to renounce their faith" (*ibid.* 607).

"The last great warning had sounded everywhere, and it had stirred up and enraged the inhabitants of the earth who would not receive the message" (EW 279).

How extensively will the knowledge of salvation be diffused?

"During the loud cry, the church, aided by the providential interpositions of her exalted Lord, will diffuse the knowledge of salvation so abundantly that light will be communicated to every city and town. The earth will be filled with the knowledge of salvation. So abundantly will the renewing Spirit of God have crowned with success the intensely active agencies, that the light of present truth will be seen flashing everywhere" (Ev 694).

"A crisis is right upon us. We must now by the Holy Spirit's power proclaim the great truths for these last days.

It will not be long before everyone will have heard the warning and made his decision. Then shall the end come" (Ev 703).

Are God's people supposed to withdraw from the Seventh-day Adventist Church and join some purer, holier group at the time of the loud cry?

"How is it that these pamphlets denouncing the Seventh-day Adventist Church as Babylon were scattered abroad everywhere, at the very time when that church was receiving the outpouring of the Spirit of God? How is it that men can be so deceived as to imagine that the loud cry consists in calling the people of God out from the fellowship of a church that is enjoying a season of refreshing?" (TM 23).

"You will take passages in the Testimonies that speak of the close of probation, of the shaking among God's people, and you will talk of a coming out from this people of a purer, holier people that will arise. Now all this pleases the enemy. . . . Should many accept the views you advance, and talk and act upon them, we would see one of the greatest fanatical excitements that has ever been witnessed among Seventh-day Adventists. This is what Satan wants" (1SM 179).

"We cannot now enter into any new organization; for this would mean apostasy from the truth" (2SM 390).

Will the loud cry come as a result of any human planning?

"Let me tell you that the Lord will work in this last work in a manner very much out of the common order of things, and in a way that will be contrary to any human planning. There will be those among us who will always want to control the work of God, to dictate even what movements shall be made when the work goes forward under the direction of the angel who joins the third angel in the message to be given to the world. God will use ways and means by which it will be seen that He is taking the reins in His own hands. The workers will be surprised by the simple means that He will use to bring about and perfect His work of righteousness" (TM 300).

"The laborers will be qualified rather by the unction of His Spirit than by the training of literary institutions. Men of faith and prayer will be constrained to go forth with holy zeal, declaring the words which God gives them" (GC 606 [see also Ev 700]).

"Many, even among the uneducated, now proclaim the words of the Lord. Children are impelled by the Spirit to go forth and declare the message from heaven. The Spirit is poured out upon all who will yield to its promptings, and, casting off all man's machinery, his binding rules and cautious methods, they will declare the truth with the might of the Spirit's power" (Ev 700).

"To souls that are earnestly seeking for light and that accept with gladness every ray of divine illumination from His holy Word, to such alone light will be given. It is through these souls that God will reveal that light and power which will lighten the whole earth with His glory" (5T 729).

"When divine power is combined with human effort, the work will spread like fire in the stubble. God will employ agencies whose origin man will be unable to discern; angels will do a work which men might have had the blessing of accomplishing, had they not neglected to answer the claims of God" (RH Dec. 15, 1885).

CHAPTER 13

THE TIMES AND THE SEASONS

Do we know the exact time the latter rain will be poured out?

"I have no specific time of which to speak when the outpouring of the Holy Spirit will take place—when the mighty angel will come down from heaven, and unite with the third angel in closing up the work for this world; my message is that our only safety is in being ready for the heavenly refreshing, having our lamps trimmed and burning" (1SM 192 [7BC 984]).

What did Jesus say about the date of His return?

Matt. 24:36; John 21:22, 23; Acts 1:6, 7.

Why has the knowledge of the time of Christ's return been withheld from us?

"Why has not God given us this knowledge? Because we would not make a right use of it if He did. A condition of things would result from this knowledge among our people that would greatly retard the work of God in preparing a people to stand in the great day that is to come. We are not to be engrossed with speculation in regard to the times and the seasons which God has not revealed" (Ev 221 [RH Mar. 22, 1892]).

What indications are there that Jesus was prepared to return to this world at some time shortly after 1844, when the last time prophecy ended?

"I saw that those who of late have embraced the truth

would have to know what it is to suffer for Christ's sake, that they would have trials to pass through that would be keen and cutting in order that they may be purified and fitted through suffering to receive the seal of the living God, pass through the time of trouble, see the King in His beauty, and dwell in the presence of God and of pure, holy angels. . . .

"I was shown the company present at the conference. Said the angel, 'Some food for worms, some subjects of the seven last plagues, some will be alive and remain upon the earth to be translated at the coming of Jesus'" (1T 131, 132 [1856]).

What was the purpose of the Laodicean message that began to be preached in 1856 among the Sabbath-keeping Adventists?

"I saw that this message would not accomplish its work in a few short months. It is designed to arouse the people of God, to discover to them their backslidings, and to lead to zealous repentance, that they may be favored with the presence of Jesus, and be fitted for the loud cry of the third angel" (1T 186 [1859]).

Did this message accomplish its purpose?

"God's people are not prepared for the loud cry of the third angel" (1T 486 [1867]).

Why did Jesus not return at once anyway? (See Jonah 3:4-10; Jer. 18:7-10.)

"The long night of gloom is trying, but the morning is deferred in mercy, because if the Master should come, so many would be found unready" (Ev 694 [2T 194 (1868)]).

Nevertheless, did Sister White believe that the Lord's coming was imminent?

"Because time is short, we should work with diligence

and double energy. Our children may never enter college" (3T 159 [1872]).

Why did Jesus not return in the years before 1883?

"Had Adventists, after the great disappointment in 1844, held fast their faith and followed on unitedly in the opening providence of God, receiving the message of the third angel and in the power of the Holy Spirit proclaiming it to the world, they would have seen the salvation of God, the Lord would have wrought mightily with their efforts, the work would have been completed, and Christ would have come ere this to receive His people to their reward. . . . It was not the will of God that the coming of Christ should be thus delayed. . . . For forty years did unbelief, murmuring, and rebellion shut out ancient Israel from the land of Canaan. The same sins have delayed the entrance of modern Israel into the heavenly Canaan. In neither case were the promises of God at fault. It is the unbelief, the worldliness, unconsecration, and strife among the Lord's professed people that have kept us in this world of sin and sorrow so many years" (Ev 695, 696 [1883]).

"If all who had labored unitedly in the work of 1844, had received the third angel's message, and proclaimed it in the power of the Holy Spirit, the Lord would have wrought mightily with their efforts. A flood of light would have been shed upon the world. Years ago the inhabitants of the earth would have been warned, the closing work completed, and Christ would have come for the redemption of His people" (4SP 291 [1884] [GC 458; 8T 116]).

In spite of the delay up to that point, what was still the prophet's expectancy?

"The Lifegiver's voice has not yet called the sleeping saints from their gloomy prisons, but we have not lost faith, because the predicted hour has not yet arrived. . . . The hour will come; it is not far distant, and some of us who now believe will be alive upon the earth, and shall see the prediction verified, and hear the voice of the archangel, and the trump of God echo from mountain and plain and sea, to the uttermost parts of the earth. All creation will hear that voice, and those who have lived and died in Jesus, will respond to the call of the Prince of life" (RH July 31, 1888).

"In this age of the world, as the scenes of earth's history are soon to close and we are about to enter upon the time of trouble such as never was, the fewer the marriages contracted, the better for all, both men and women" (5T 366 [1885]).

What message, proclaimed with power in the three years following the 1888 General Conference session, was the "beginning" of the loud cry?

"The time of test is just upon us, for the loud cry of the third angel has already begun in the revelation of the righteousness of Christ, the sin-pardoning Redeemer. This is the beginning of the light of the angel whose glory shall fill the whole earth" (1SM 363 [7BC 984; RH Nov. 22, 1892]).

Was the latter rain falling on God's people in 1892, or was this just the "swelling" of the message that eventually would become the loud cry?

"We are not to know the definite time either for the outpouring of the Holy Spirit or for the coming of Christ. . . . The third angel's message is swelling into a loud cry. . . . Today you are to have your vessel purified that it may be ready for the heavenly dew, ready for the showers of the latter rain; for the latter rain will come, and the blessing of God will fill every soul that is purified from every defilement. It is our work today to yield our souls to Christ, that we may be fitted for the time of refreshing from the presence of the Lord—fitted for the baptism of the Holy Spirit" (RH Mar. 22, 1892).

What was Sister White's attitude, in 1891, concerning the nearness of Christ's return?

"You will not be able to say that He will come in one, two, or five years, neither are you to put off His coming by stating that it may not be for ten or twenty years" (RH Mar. 22, 1892 [Ev 221]).

Why did Jesus further delay His second advent?

"Had the church of Christ done her appointed work as the Lord ordained, the whole world would before this have been warned, and the Lord Jesus would have come to our earth in power and great glory" (DA 633, 634 [1898]).

"Had the purpose of God been carried out by His people in giving to the world the message of mercy, Christ would, ere this, have come to the earth, and the saints would have received their welcome into the city of God" (6T 450 [1900]).

"The lesson of this record is for us. The Lord had prepared the way before His people. They were very near the promised land. A little while and they would have entered Canaan. They themselves delayed the entering. . . . Had they put their trust in God, they could have gone straight in. God would have gone before them. . . . Brethren and sisters, from the light given me, I know that if the people of God had preserved a living connection with Him, if they had obeyed His Word, they could today be in the heavenly Canaan" (GCB Mar. 30, 1903 [see also Ev 694]).

Whose fault is it that we are in this sinful world, and that Jesus has not yet returned?

"We may have to remain here in this world because of

insubordination many more years, as did the children of Israel; but for Christ's sake, His people should not add sin to sin by charging God with the consequence of their own wrong course of action" (Ev 696 [1901]).

What is Christ waiting for?

"When the character of Christ shall be perfectly reproduced in His people, then He will come to claim them as His own. It is the privilege of every Christian not only to look for but to hasten the coming of our Lord Jesus Christ" (COL 69).

How do Mrs. White's expectations of the return of Christ compare with those of the Bible prophets?

Rev. 22:6, 7, 12, 20; 1 Cor. 7:29; Rom. 13:11, 12.

"The angels of God in their messages to men represent time as very short. Thus it has always been presented to me. It is true that time has continued longer than we expected in the early days of this message. Our Saviour did not appear as soon as we hoped. But has the word of the Lord failed? Never! It should be remembered that the promises and threatenings of God are alike conditional" (1SM 67).

What should our attitude be today?

"Instead of exhausting the powers of our mind in speculations in regard to the times and seasons which the Lord has placed in His own power, and withheld from men, we are to yield ourselves to the control of the Holy Spirit, to do present duties, to give the bread of life, unadulterated by human opinions, to souls who are perishing for the truth" (Ev 702 [6BC 1052; RH Mar. 22, 1892]).

THE SEAL OF GOD

What special event is described as taking place shortly before the close of probation?

Rev. 7:1-4. Eze. 9:1-6.

"John sees the elements of nature—earthquake, tempest, and political strife—represented as being held by four angels. These winds are under control until God gives the word to let them go. There is the safety of God's church. The angels of God do His bidding, holding back the winds of the earth, that the winds should not blow on the earth, nor on the sea, nor on any tree, until the servants of God should be sealed in their foreheads. . . . This sealing of the servants of God is the same that was shown to Ezekiel in vision" (TM 444, 445).

What is the seal of the living God?

Ex. 20:8-11; 31:12-17.

"Too late they see that the Sabbath of the fourth commandment is the seal of the living God" (GC 640).

"True observance of the Sabbath is the sign of loyalty to God" (7BC 981).

"Those who would have the seal of God in their foreheads must keep the Sabbath of the fourth commandment" (*ibid.* 970).

"There is to be a mark placed upon God's people, and that mark is the keeping of His holy Sabbath" (*ibid.* 981).

"To us as to Israel the Sabbath is given 'for a perpetual covenant.' To those who reverence His holy day the

Sabbath is a sign that God recognizes them as His chosen people. It is a pledge that He will fulfill to them His covenant. Every soul who accepts the sign of God's government places himself under the divine, everlasting covenant. He fastens himself to the golden chain of obedience, every link of which is a promise.

"The fourth commandment alone of all the ten contains the seal of the great Lawgiver, the Creator of the heavens and the earth" (6T 350 [see also PP 307]).

What must be the spiritual condition of all who receive the seal of God's approval?

They will have perfect characters. "Are we seeking for His fullness, ever pressing toward the mark set before us—the perfection of His character? When the Lord's people reach this mark, they will be sealed in their foreheads. Filled with the Spirit, they will be complete in Christ, and the recording angel will declare, 'It is finished'" (6BC 1118).

Nothing can move them from the truth. "Just as soon as the people of God are sealed in their foreheads—it is not any seal or mark that can be seen, but a settling into the truth, both intellectually and spiritually, so they cannot be moved—just as soon as God's people are sealed and prepared for the shaking, it will come. Indeed, it has begun already; the judgments of God are now upon the land, to give us warning, that we may know what is coming" (4BC 1161).

They are Christlike. "The seal of the living God will be placed upon those only who bear a likeness to Christ in character" (7BC 970).

They are overcomers. "Those that overcome the world, the flesh, and the devil, will be the favored ones who shall receive the seal of the living God" (TM 445).

They are pure and without spot. "Now is the time to prepare. The seal of God will never be placed upon the forehead of an impure man or woman. It will never be placed on the forehead of the ambitious, world-loving man or woman. It will never be placed upon the forehead of men or women of false tongues or deceitful hearts. All who receive the seal must be without spot before God—candidates for heaven" (5T 216).

They mourn over their own sins and sins in the church and world. "At the time when the danger and depression of the church are greatest, the little company who are standing in the light will be sighing and crying for the abominations that are done in the land. But more especially will their prayers arise in behalf of the church because its members are doing after the manner of the world. . . . They lament and afflict their souls because pride, avarice, selfishness, and deception of almost every kind are in the church. . . . The class who do not feel grieved over their own spiritual declension, nor mourn over the sins of others, will be left without the seal of God. . . . The seal of God will be placed upon the foreheads of those only who sigh and cry for the abominations done in the land" (*ibid.* 209-212).

"Only those who, in their attitude before God, are filling the position of those who are repenting and confessing their sins in the great antitypical day of atonement, will be recognized and marked as worthy of God's protection" (TM 445).

Are we in the sealing time now? If so, when did it begin?

"I saw that the present test on the Sabbath could not come until the mediation of Jesus in the holy place was finished and He had passed within the second veil; therefore Christians who fell asleep before the door was opened into the most holy, when the midnight cry was finished, at the seventh month, 1844, and who had not kept the true

Sabbath, now rest in hope; for they had not the light and the test on the Sabbath which we now have since that door was opened. I saw that Satan was tempting some of God's people on this point. Because so many good Christians have fallen asleep in the triumphs of faith and have not kept the true Sabbath, they were doubting about its being a test for us now. . . . Satan is now using every device in this sealing time to keep the minds of God's people from the present truth and to cause them to waver" (EW 42, 43).

"The sealing time is very short, and will soon be over. Now is the time, while the four angels are holding the four winds, to make our calling and election sure" (EW 58).

Do we know of any people who have already been sealed?

"I saw that she [Mrs. Hastings] was sealed and would come up at the voice of God and stand upon the earth, and would be with the 144,000. I saw we need not mourn for her; she would rest in the time of trouble" (2SM 263).

"There are living upon our earth men who have passed the age of fourscore and ten. The natural results of old age are seen in their feebleness. But they believe God, and God loves them. The seal of God is upon them, and they will be among the number of whom the Lord has said, 'Blessed are the dead which die in the Lord'" (7BC 982).

Is it possible that there are men and women living today who have already received the seal of God?

"Another 'suppression' reads as follows: 'Well, bless the Lord, brethren and sisters, it is an extra meeting for those that have the seal of the living God.' There is nothing in this that we do not still hold. Reference to our published works will show our belief that the living righteous will receive the seal of God prior to the close of probation;

also that these will enjoy special honors in the kingdom of God" (1SM 66).

Before the sealing of God's people is finished, what glorious event will take place?

"Before the work is closed up and the sealing of God's people is finished, we shall receive the outpouring of the Spirit of God" (1SM 111).

"Not one of us will ever receive the seal of God while our characters have one spot or stain upon them. It is left with us to remedy the defects in our characters, to cleanse the soul temple of every defilement. Then the latter rain will fall upon us as the early rain fell upon the disciples on the day of Pentecost" (5T 214).

What will happen to those who are not settled "into the truth . . . so they cannot be moved"?

"Just as soon as the people of God are sealed in their foreheads—it is not any seal or mark that can be seen, but a settling into the truth, both intellectually and spiritually, so they cannot be moved—just as soon as God's people are sealed and prepared for the shaking, it will come. Indeed, it has begun already; the judgments of God are now upon the land, to give us warning, that we may know what is coming" (4BC 1161).

What universal decree will be passed before all of God's people are sealed?

"The powers of earth, uniting to war against the commandments of God, will decree that 'all, both small and great, rich and poor, free and bond' (Rev. 13:16), shall conform to the customs of the church by the observance of the false sabbath. . . . On the other hand, the law of God enjoining the Creator's rest day demands obedience and threatens wrath against all who transgress its precepts. With the issue thus clearly brought before him, whoever shall trample upon God's law to obey a human enactment receives the mark of the beast" (GC 604).

"When you obey the decree that commands you to cease from labor on Sunday . . . you consent to receive the mark of the beast, and refuse the seal of God. If we receive this mark in our foreheads or in our hands, the judgments pronounced against the disobedient must fall upon us. But the seal of the living God is placed upon those who conscientiously keep the Sabbath of the Lord" (RH July 13, 1897 [7BC 980]).

"The Lord has shown me clearly that the image of the beast will be formed before probation closes; for it is to be the great test for the people of God, by which their eternal destiny will be decided. . . . [Rev. 13:11-17 quoted.] . . .

"This is the test that the people of God must have before they are sealed. All who prove their loyalty to God by observing His law, and refusing to accept a spurious sabbath, will rank under the banner of the Lord God Jehovah, and will receive the seal of the living God. Those who yield the truth of heavenly origin and accept the Sunday sabbath will receive the mark of the beast" (7BC 976).

What is "the number of them which were sealed"?
Rev. 7:4.

Do we know whether this is a literal number or a figurative number?

"It is not His will that they shall get into controversy over questions which will not help them spiritually, such as, Who is to compose the hundred and forty-four thousand? This those who are the elect of God will in a short time know without question" (1SM 174).

When the sealing angel has finished his work, what will Jesus do?

"An angel returning from the earth announces that his work is done; the final test has been brought upon the world, and all who have proved themselves loyal to the divine precepts have received 'the seal of the living God.' Then Jesus ceases His intercession in the sanctuary above" (GC 613).

"I saw angels hurrying to and fro in heaven. An angel with a writer's inkhorn by his side returned from the earth and reported to Jesus that his work was done, and the saints were numbered and sealed. Then I saw Jesus, who had been ministering before the ark containing the ten commandments, throw down the censer. He raised His hands, and with a loud voice said, *'It is done.'* And all the angelic host laid off their crowns as Jesus made the solemn declaration, 'He that is unjust, let him be unjust still; and he which is filthy, let him be filthy still; and he that is righteous, let him be righteous still; and he that is holy, let him be holy still'" (EW 279, 280).

Then what will the four angels do?

"Just before we entered it [the time of trouble], we all received the seal of the living God. Then I saw the four angels cease to hold the four winds. And I saw famine, pestilence and sword, nation rose against nation, and the whole world was in confusion" (7BC 968).

Who only will be protected in the time of trouble?

"Those who receive the seal of the living God and are protected in the time of trouble must reflect the image of Jesus fully" (EW 71).

Will the seal of God be placed upon us?

"In a little while every one who is a child of God will

have His seal placed upon him. O that it may be placed upon our foreheads! Who can endure the thought of being forever passed by when the angel goes forth to seal the servants of God in their foreheads?" (RH May 28, 1889).

"Our own course of action will determine whether we shall receive the seal of the living God or be cut down by the destroying weapons. Already a few drops of God's wrath have fallen upon the earth; but when the seven last plagues shall be poured out without mixture into the cup of His indignation, then it will be forever too late to repent and find shelter. No atoning blood will then wash away the stains of sin.

" 'And at that time shall Michael stand up.' . . . Every case is decided; there is no longer probation, no longer mercy for the impenitent. The seal of the living God is upon His people" (5T 212, 213).

THE MARK OF THE BEAST

How does John the revelator warn us against receiving the mark of the beast?

Rev. 14:9, 10; 16:2.

How will Satan threaten those who refuse the mark of the beast?

Rev. 13:11, 15-17.

What is the mark of the beast?

"John was called to behold a people distinct from those who worship the beast or his image by keeping the first day of the week. The observance of this day is the mark of the beast" (TM 133).

"The sign, or seal, of God is revealed in the observance of the seventh-day Sabbath, the Lord's memorial of Creation. . . . The mark of the beast is the opposite of this—the observance of the first day of the week" (8T 117).

"The mark of the beast is the papal sabbath" (Ev 234).

"When the test comes, it will be clearly shown what the mark of the beast is. It is the keeping of Sunday" (7BC 980).

"Sundaykeeping is not yet the mark of the beast, and will not be until the decree goes forth causing men to worship this idol sabbath. The time will come when this day will be the test, but that time has not come yet" (*ibid.* 977 [1899]).

How many people did Mrs. White say had the mark of the beast?

"No one has yet received the mark of the beast" (Ev 234 [1899]).

When will the mark of the beast be received? Will this be before or after the close of probation? Will it be possible for anyone to slip past the close of probation without receiving either the seal of God or the mark of the beast?

"The testing time has not yet come. There are true Christians in every church, not excepting the Roman Catholic communion. None are condemned until they have had the light and have seen the obligation of the fourth commandment. But when the decree shall go forth enforcing the counterfeit sabbath, and the loud cry of the third angel shall warn men against the worship of the beast and his image, the line will be clearly drawn between the false and the true. Then those who still continue in transgression will receive the mark of the beast" (Ev 234, 235).

"If the light of truth has been presented to you, revealing the Sabbath of the fourth commandment, and showing that there is no foundation in the Word of God for Sunday observance, and yet you still cling to the false sabbath, refusing to keep holy the Sabbath which God calls 'My holy day,' you receive the mark of the beast. When does this take place? When you obey the decree that commands you to cease from labor on Sunday and worship God, while you know that there is not a word in the Bible showing Sunday to be other than a common working day, you consent to receive the mark of the beast, and refuse the seal of God.

"If we receive this mark in our foreheads or in our hands, the judgments pronounced against the disobedient must fall upon us. But the seal of the living God is placed upon those who conscientiously keep the Sabbath of the Lord" (RH July 13, 1897 [7BC 980; see also Ev 235]).

"When Sunday observance shall be enforced by law, and the world shall be enlightened concerning the obligation of the true Sabbath, then whoever shall transgress the command of God, to obey a precept which has no higher authority than that of Rome, will thereby honor popery above God. He is paying homage to Rome and to the power which enforces the institution ordained by Rome. He is worshiping the beast and his image. As men then reject the institution which God has declared to be the sign of His authority, and honor in its stead that which Rome has chosen as the token of her supremacy, they will thereby accept the sign of allegiance to Rome—'the mark of the beast.' And it is not until the issue is thus plainly set before the people, and they are brought to choose between the commandments of God and the commandments of men, that those who continue in transgression will receive 'the mark of the beast'" (GC 449).

"The powers of earth, uniting to war against the commandments of God, will decree that 'all, both small and great, rich and poor, free and bond' (Rev. 13:16), shall conform to the customs of the church by the observance of the false sabbath. . . . On the other hand, the law of God enjoining the Creator's rest day demands obedience and threatens wrath against all who transgress its precepts.

"While one class, by accepting the sign of submission to earthly powers, receive the mark of the beast, the other choosing the token of allegiance to divine authority, receive the seal of God" (*ibid.* 605).

THE CLOSE OF PROBATION

Are there some people living today who have closed their individual probation, so that the Holy Spirit can no longer reach them?

"Every day the probation of some is closing. Every hour some are passing beyond the reach of mercy" (PP 140).

"Every day we have been associating with men and women who are judgment bound. Each day may have been the dividing line to some soul; someone may have made the decision which will determine his future destiny. What has been our influence over these fellow travelers? What efforts have we put forth to bring them to Christ?" (5T 466).

Do we know when our own period of probation may close?

"We know not how soon our probation may close. At the longest, we have but a brief lifetime here, and we know not how soon the arrow of death may strike our hearts. We know not how soon we may be called to give up the world and all its interests" (MH 454).

Upon what four occasions, at least, in the past has there been a general close of probation for a large number of people?

"There was a shut door in Noah's day. There was at that time a withdrawal of the Spirit of God from the sinful race that perished in the waters of the Flood" (1SM 63).

"There was a shut door in the days of Abraham. Mercy

ceased to plead with the inhabitants of Sodom" *(ibid.)*.

"There was a shut door in Christ's day. The Son of God declared to the unbelieving Jews of that generation, 'Your house is left unto you desolate' (Matt. 23:38)" *(ibid.)*.

"There was a shut door in 1844. All who saw the light of the first and second angels' messages and rejected that light were left in darkness. And those who accepted it and received the Holy Spirit which attended the proclamation of the message from heaven, and who afterward renounced their faith and pronounced their experience a delusion, thereby rejected the Spirit of God, and it no longer pleaded with them" *(ibid.)*.

What divine decree will close the time of probation for the entire human family?
Rev. 22:11, 12.

What act of Christ will indicate that His intercession in behalf of sinners is forever finished?
Dan. 12:1; Rev. 15:8.

Do we know when that fateful hour will come?
"God has not revealed to us the time when this message will close, or when probation will have an end. Those things that are revealed we shall accept for ourselves and for our children; but let us not seek to know that which has been kept secret in the councils of the Almighty" (1SM 191 [7BC 989]).

"Letters have come to me asking me if I have any special light as to the time when probation will close; and I answer that I have only this message to bear, that it is now time to work while the day lasts, for the night cometh in which no man can work" *(ibid.)*.

"There is no command for anyone to search the

Scriptures in order to ascertain, if possible, when probation will close. God has no such message for any mortal lips. He would have no mortal tongue declare that which He has hidden in His secret councils" (1SM 192 [7BC 990]).

Are there any time prophecies that must yet be fulfilled before probation can close?

"The people will not have another message upon definite time. . . . The longest reckoning reaches to the autumn of 1844" (7BC 971).

What definite prediction is made concerning the enforcement of Sunday observance before the close of probation?

"The Lord has shown me clearly that the image of the beast will be formed before probation closes; for it is to be the great test for the people of God, by which their eternal destiny will be decided. . . . This is the test that the people of God must have before they are sealed" (7BC 976).

"The great final test comes at the close of human probation, when it will be too late for the soul's need to be supplied" (COL 412).

What is the relationship between the universal Sunday law and the close of probation for the nations of earth?

(See p. 37, "What relationship does the universal Sunday law bear to the close of probation?")

What three tasks are completed almost simultaneously at the close of probation?

"The people of God have accomplished their work. . . . An angel returning from the earth announces that his work is done. . . . Then Jesus ceases His intercession in the sanctuary above. He lifts His hands and with a loud voice says, 'It is done'" (GC 613).

"Reference to our published works will show our belief that the living righteous will receive the seal of God prior to the close of probation; also that these will enjoy special honors in the kingdom of God" (1SM 66).

"When the work of investigation shall be ended, when the cases of those who in all ages have professed to be followers of Christ have been examined and decided, then, and not till then, probation will close, and the door of mercy will be shut" (GC 428).

What will life be like in this world on the day that probation closes? Will anyone be aware that the decisive hour has come?

"Before the Flood, after Noah entered the ark, God shut him in and shut the ungodly out; but for seven days the people, knowing not that their doom was fixed, continued their careless, pleasure-loving life and mocked the warnings of impending judgment. 'So,' says the Saviour, 'shall also the coming of the Son of man be' (Matt. 24:39). Silently, unnoticed as the midnight thief, will come the decisive hour which marks the fixing of every man's destiny, the final withdrawal of mercy's offer to guilty men" (GC 491).

"While the man of business is absorbed in the pursuit of gain, while the pleasure lover is seeking indulgence, while the daughter of fashion is arranging her adornments—it may be in that hour the Judge of all the earth will pronounce the sentence: 'Thou art weighed in the balances, and art found wanting'" *(ibid.)*.

"The crisis is stealing gradually upon us. The sun shines in the heavens, passing over its usual round, and the heavens still declare the glory of God. Men are still eating and drinking, planting and building, marrying and giving in marriage. Merchants are still buying and selling. Men are jostling one against another, contending for the highest place. Pleasure lovers are still crowding to theaters, horse races, gambling hells. The highest excitement prevails, yet probation's hour is fast closing, and every case is about to be eternally decided. Satan sees that his time is short. He has set all his agencies at work that men may be deceived, deluded, occupied, and entranced until the day of probation shall be ended, and the door of mercy forever shut" (ChS 51 [see also FE 335]).

What will life continue to be like right up to the moment of the destruction of the wicked?

"As the people of Noah's day 'knew not until the flood came, and took them all away; so,' in the words of our Saviour, 'shall also the coming of the Son of man be' (Matt. 24:39). When the professed people of God are uniting with the world, living as they live, and joining with them in forbidden pleasures; when the luxury of the world becomes the luxury of the church; when the marriage bells are chiming, and all are looking forward to many years of worldly prosperity—then, suddenly as the lightning flashes from the heavens, will come the end of their bright visions and delusive hopes" (GC 338, 339).

"When the reasoning of philosophy has banished the fear of God's judgments; when religious teachers are pointing forward to long ages of peace and prosperity, and the world are absorbed in their rounds of business and pleasure, planting and building, feasting and merrymaking, rejecting God's warnings and mocking His messengers—then it is that sudden destruction cometh upon them, and they shall not escape (1 Thess. 5:3)" (PP 104).

"Come when it may, the day of God will come unawares to the ungodly. When life is going on in its unvarying round; when men are absorbed in pleasure, in business, in traffic, in money-making; when religious leaders are magnifying the world's progress and enlightenment, and the people are lulled in a false security—then, as the midnight thief steals within the unguarded dwelling, so shall sudden destruction come upon the careless and ungodly, 'and they shall not escape' (1 Thess. 5:3)" (GC 38).

"The forms of religion will be continued by a people from whom the Spirit of God has been finally withdrawn; and the satanic zeal with which the prince of evil will inspire them for the accomplishment of his malignant designs will bear the semblance of zeal for God" (*ibid.* 615).

Will Seventh-day Adventists expect probation to close when it does?

"The solemn fact is to be kept not only before the people of the world, but before our own churches also, that the day of the Lord will come suddenly, unexpectedly" (FE 336).

"When probation ends, it will come suddenly, unexpectedly—at a time when we are least expecting it. But we can have a clean record in heaven today, and know that God accepts us" (7BC 989).

Where will the righteous be living and what will they be doing up to the time of probation's close?

"The wheat and tares 'grow together until the harvest.' In the discharge of life's duties the righteous will to the last be brought in contact with the ungodly. The children of light are scattered among the children of darkness, that the contrast may be seen by all" (5T 100).

Will there be any supernatural sign on earth to

indicate that Christ has finished His intercessory ministry in heaven?

G. A. Irwin wrote in the *Review and Herald Supplement* of June 21, 1898, "A darkness will cover the inhabitants of the earth when Jesus moves out of the heavenly sanctuary, such as enveloped the earth at the time of the crucifixion" (p. 1). It should be clearly understood, however, that there is no Spirit of Prophecy support for this statement. Sister White says, "When He leaves the sanctuary, darkness covers the inhabitants of the earth" (GC 614). This darkness is no doubt spiritual, the "darkness of error and delusion" (EW 104).

Will the righteous have any other way of knowing that probation has closed?

"When the irrevocable decision of the sanctuary has been pronounced and the destiny of the world has been forever fixed, the inhabitants of the earth will know it not" (GC 615).

"The righteous and the wicked will still be living upon the earth in their mortal state—men will be planting and building, eating and drinking, all unconscious that the final, irrevocable decision has been pronounced in the sanctuary above" (*ibid.* 491).

Will Satan know that probation has closed?

"In the time of trouble, Satan stirs up the wicked, and they encircle the people of God to destroy them. But he does not know that 'pardon' has been written opposite their names in the books of heaven" (RH Nov. 19, 1908).

"He sees that holy angels are guarding [the people of God], and he infers that their sins have been pardoned; but he does not know that their cases have been decided in the sanctuary above" (GC 618).

What does the Bible say will follow probation's close?
Rev. 15:8; 16:1; 19:11-15.

"I saw that the four angels would hold the four winds until Jesus' work was done in the sanctuary, and then will come the seven last plagues" (EW 36).

"When the work of the investigative judgment closes, the destiny of all will have been decided for life or death. Probation is ended a short time before the appearing of the Lord in the clouds of heaven" (GC 490).

PERFECTION IN CHRIST

How holy, or righteous, are we at birth?

Job 14:4; Ps. 51:5; Rom. 3:10, 19.

"Adam was created a pure, sinless being, without a taint of sin upon him; he was in the image of God. He could fall, and he did fall through transgressing. Because of sin his posterity was born with inherent propensities of disobedience" (5BC 1128).

How many have yielded to their natural propensities to wrong?

Rom. 3:23.

How perfect, or holy, must we be if we are to be saved in God's kingdom?

Heb. 12:14.

"He who enters heaven must have a character that is without spot or wrinkle or any such thing. Naught that defileth can ever enter there. In all the redeemed host not one defect will be seen" (MYP 144).

What provision has the Lord made so that the gap between His perfect requirements and our imperfect lives may be bridged?

Rom. 5:17-19; 1 Peter 2:24.

"Christ was treated as we deserve, that we might be treated as He deserves. He was condemned for our sins, in which He had no share, that we might be justified by

His righteousness, in which we had no share. He suffered the death which was ours, that we might receive the life which was His. 'With His stripes we are healed'" (DA 25).

How can sinners avail themselves of heaven's Gift?
Rom. 3:24-28.

"The only way in which [a sinner] can attain to righteousness is through faith. By faith [the sinner] can bring to God the merits of Christ, and the Lord places the obedience of His Son to the sinner's account" (1SM 367).

After Christ forgives our sins and covers us with His robe of righteousness, how perfect or holy are we in God's sight?
Rom. 4:5-7.

"Through the righteousness of Christ we shall stand before God pardoned, and as though we had never sinned" (5BC 1142).

"Through the efficacy of Christ's sacrifice we may stand before God pure and spotless, our sins atoned for and pardoned. . . . The redeemed sinner, clothed in the robes of Christ's righteousness, may stand in the presence of a sin-hating God, made perfect by the merits of the Saviour" (RH May 5, 1910).

"Jesus continues: As you confess Me before men, so I will confess you before God and the holy angels. You are to be My witnesses upon earth, channels through which My grace can flow for the healing of the world. So I will be your representative in heaven. The Father beholds not your faulty character, but He sees you as clothed in My perfection" (DA 357).

Even though, in one sense, we may be considered

perfect at conversion, what is the next part of God's plan for us?

1 Thess. 4:3.

"To restore in man the image of his Maker, to bring him back to the perfection in which he was created, to promote the development of body, mind, and soul, that the divine purpose in his creation might be realized—this was to be the work of redemption. This is the object of education, the great object of life" (Ed 15, 16).

"God's ideal for His children is higher than the highest human thought can reach. 'Be ye therefore perfect, even as your Father which is in heaven is perfect.' This command is a promise. The plan of redemption contemplates our complete recovery from the power of Satan. Christ always separates the contrite soul from sin" (DA 311).

"When souls are converted, their salvation is not yet accomplished. They then have the race to run; the arduous struggle is before them to 'fight the good fight of faith.' . . . The battle is lifelong, and must be carried forward with determined energy proportionate to the value of the object you are in pursuit of, which is eternal life" (OHC 163).

"The work of sanctification must go on, not by impulse, but by steady, healthy advances, progressing toward perfection" (RH Mar. 5, 1895).

"The righteousness by which we are justified is imputed; the righteousness by which we are sanctified is imparted. The first is our title to heaven, the second is our fitness for heaven" (MYP 35).

During our experience as a Christian, does the Lord regard us as perfect or imperfect—or both?

Perfect. A new-born Christian is perfect just as a newly born baby is perfect. Jesus has forgiven our sins. We are justified through the imputed righteousness of Christ. The thief on the cross, from this standpoint, was perfect. See quotations on page 142 under the question "After Christ forgives our sins and covers us with His robe of righteousness, how perfect or holy are we in God's sight?"

The Lord considers the growing Christian to be perfect if He is satisfied with his development. We may have been Christians for just a little while, our understanding of spiritual things may be only partial, and our faith weak, but God still will consider us perfect if we are maturing steadily through the imparted righteousness of Christ. "At every stage of development our life may be perfect; yet if God's purpose for us is fulfilled, there will be continual advancement" (COL 65). In spite of their faults the Bible calls Noah, Hezekiah, and Asa perfect (Gen. 6:9; Isa. 38:3; 1 Kings 15:14). Paul speaks of those in his day who were perfect (Phil. 3:15), but in the same breath says that it was not the highest perfection attainable (verse12). (See page 146, the first two quotations under the question "When Jesus said, 'Be ye therefore perfect,' what did He mean?".)

The Christian is also considered perfect when, through the imparted righteousness of Christ, he reaches the place where he does not sin, even by a thought. Such a one, through the divine power supplied him, has reached the highest goal of perfection attainable in this life. At the close of probation every one of the living saints will, by God's grace, have achieved this level of spirituality. (See quotations on page [156], under the question "Under the power of the perfecting latter rain, to what spiritual state will God's people—the 144,000—be brought by the close of probation?")

Imperfect. The thief on the cross and all new converts may be thought of as imperfect in that they have had no opportunity to develop their characters. There is a lifetime of improvement to make.

A Christian of many years experience is certainly imperfect while he continues to sin, even occasionally. David was a man after God's own heart but he was also very imperfect. "We are not yet perfect; but it is our privilege to cut away from the entanglements of self and sin, and advance to perfection" (AA 565).

The Christian who ceases to sin, even by a thought, is imperfect in the sense that there is still much more that he can learn about God. "Even the most perfect Christian may increase continually in the knowledge and love of God" (1T 340). "By growing daily in the divine life, he will not attain to the full stature of a perfect man in Christ until his probation ceases" (4T 367).

The Christian who does not sin, even by a thought, is still subject to the temptations of his lower nature. He still has the battle to fight, and must do so until the moment of Christ's return. He is imperfect and will be until Christ gives him a new body with all natural propensities to sin removed. "We cannot say, "I am sinless," till this vile body is changed and fashioned like unto His glorious body" (ST Mar. 23, 1888). See quotations on pages 157 and 158, "Will they still feel the promptings of sin and be tempted after probation has closed?" and "When will all temptation cease?"

The Christian who ceases to sin, even by a thought, is still a human being, capable of making unintentional mistakes. He might use poor grammar and might even have some unpleasant personality traits or habits of personal hygiene. His character may be perfect, but as a child of sinful Adam, he is imperfect. "Everything that is human is imperfect" (1SM 20). "To cast off the erring, or to treat them coldly, would not be doing as Christ has done for [us]. We are all fallible, and need the pity and consideration and forgiveness of one another. [We] cannot find perfection anywhere, and should not expect it, but . . . must bear with the perversity of men, and try to teach them" (MM 211).

When Jesus said, "Be ye therefore perfect," what did He mean?

"Christ presents before us the highest perfection of Christian character, which throughout our lifetime we should aim to reach. 'Be ye therefore perfect,' He says, 'even as your Father which is in heaven is perfect' (Matt. 5:48). Concerning this perfection, Paul writes: 'Not as though I had already attained, either were already perfect, but I follow after' (Phil. 3:12)" (MS 148, 1902).

"The apostle himself was endeavoring to reach the same standard of holiness which he set before his brethren" (SL 86).

"With our limited powers we are to be as holy in our sphere as God is holy in His sphere" (SD 155 [RH Nov. 1, 1892]).

"Our work is to strive to attain in our sphere of action the perfection that Christ in His life on the earth attained in every phase of character" (SD 154 [MM 253]).

"He is our pattern. . . . We cannot equal the pattern, but we shall not be approved of God if we do not copy it and, according to the ability which God has given, resemble it" (2T 549).

Is this objective—perfection in our sphere of action— an unattainable ideal or a goal that can actually be reached?

"Those only who through faith in Christ obey all of God's commandments will reach the condition of sinlessness in which Adam lived before his transgression. They testify to their love of Christ by obeying all His precepts" (6BC 1118).

"This example is given us that we may know the possibilities, the heights we may reach in and through Christ. The standard He presents is perfection in Him, and through His merits we may attain to it. We come short because we are content to look at earthly things rather than at heavenly" (KH 117).

"Jesus revealed no qualities, and exercised no powers, that men may not have through faith in Him. His perfect humanity is that which all His followers may possess, if they will be in subjection to God as He was" (DA 664).

"He has made it possible for them to perfect Christian character through His name and to overcome on their own account as He overcame in their behalf" (3T 365).

"God calls upon us to reach the standard of perfection and places before us the example of Christ's character. In His humanity, perfected by a life of constant resistance of evil, the Saviour showed that through cooperation with Divinity, human beings may in this life attain to perfection of character. This is God's assurance to us that we too may obtain complete victory" (AA 531).

Does the Lord intend that, by His grace, we shall live a life here and now that is free from sin?

Jude 24; Phil. 4:13; 2 Peter 2:9; 1 Cor. 10:13; 2 Cor. 10:5.

"We can overcome. Yes; fully, entirely. Jesus died to make a way of escape for us, that we might overcome every evil temper, every sin, every temptation, and sit down at last with Him" (1T 144).

"Christ died to make it possible for you to cease to sin" (RH Aug. 28, 1894).

"If you will stand under the bloodstained banner of Prince Emmanuel, faithfully doing His service, you need never yield to temptation; for One stands by your side who is able to keep you from falling" (OHC 19).

"There is no excuse for sinning. A holy temper, a Christlike life, is accessible to every repenting, believing child of God" (DA 311).

"His life testifies that it is possible for us also to obey the law of God" (*ibid.* 24).

"[Satan] is constantly seeking to deceive the followers of Christ with his fatal sophistry that it is impossible for them to overcome. . . . Let none, then, regard their defects as incurable. God will give faith and grace to overcome them" (GC 489).

"Christ came to make us 'partakers of the divine nature,' and His life declares that humanity, combined with divinity, does not commit sin" (MH 180).

"By living a sinless life He testified that every son and daughter of Adam can resist the temptations of the one who first brought sin into the world" (1SM 226).

"The strongest temptation is no excuse for sin. However great the pressure brought to bear upon the soul, transgression is our own act. It is not in the power of earth or hell to compel anyone to sin. The will must consent, the heart must yield, or passion can not overbear reason, nor iniquity triumph over righteousness" (ST Oct. 4, 1883).

"Not even by a thought did He yield to temptation. So it may be with us" (DA 123).

Does this mean that every sinful propensity within us can be subdued?

"If we consent, He will so identify Himself with our thoughts and aims, so blend our hearts and minds into conformity to His will, that when obeying Him we shall be but carrying out our own impulses" (*ibid.* 668).

"Christ came to this world and lived the law of God, that man might have perfect mastery over the natural inclinations which corrupt the soul. . . . Man may stand conqueror of himself, conqueror of his own inclinations" (MH 130, 131).

"We must learn of Christ. We must know what He is to those He has ransomed. We must realize that through belief in Him it is our privilege to be partakers of the divine nature, and so escape the corruption that is in the world through lust. Then we are cleansed from all sin, all defects of character. We need not retain one sinful propensity" (7BC 943).

"Without the transforming process which can come alone through divine power, the original propensities to sin are left in the heart in all their strength, to forge new chains, to impose a slavery that can never be broken by human power" (Ev 192).

"The propensities that control the natural heart must be subdued by the grace of Christ before fallen man is fitted to enter heaven" (AA 273).

Are Christians who do "not retain one sinful propensity" delivered from the daily struggle with these propensities? Do they cease to trouble them?

"Paul's sanctification was a constant conflict with self. Said he, 'I die daily' (1 Cor. 15:31). His will and his desires every day conflicted with duty and the will of God. Instead of following inclination, he did the will of God, however unpleasant and crucifying to his nature" (LS 237).

Do not some people have more to overcome than others, because of hereditary and environmental factors?

"While some are continually harassed, afflicted, and in trouble because of their unhappy traits of character, having to war with internal foes and the corruption of their nature, others have not half so much to battle against" (2T 74).

Does the Lord allow for these individual differences among us? Does He expect all of His children to have an identical Christian experience?

"Lead the people to look to Jesus as their only hope

and helper; leave the Lord room to work upon the mind, to speak to the soul, and to impress the understanding. It is not essential for you to know and tell others all the whys and wherefores as to what constitutes the new heart, or as to the position they can and must reach so as never to sin. You have no such work to do. All are not constituted alike. Conversions are not all alike" (1SM 177).

Can those with the strongest temptations also achieve complete victory over sin?

"Let no one say, I cannot remedy my defects of character. If you come to this decision, you will certainly fail of obtaining everlasting life. The impossibility lies in your own will" (COL 331).

"Through the plan of redemption, God has provided means for subduing every sinful trait, and resisting every temptation, however strong" (1SM 82).

Have there ever been people in the past who, through the power of the Holy Spirit, have learned to live above sin?

"The godly character of this prophet [Enoch] represents the state of holiness which must be attained by those who shall be 'redeemed from the earth' (Rev. 14:3) at the time of Christ's second advent" (PP 88, 89 [see also RH July 31, 1888]).

"Not even by a thought could our Saviour be brought to yield to the power of temptation. . . . This is the condition in which those must be found who shall stand in the time of trouble" (GC 623).

"The case of Daniel was presented before me. Although he was a man of like passions with ourselves, the pen of inspiration presents him as a faultless character. His life is given us as a bright example of what man may become, even in this life, if he will make God his strength and wisely improve the opportunities and privileges within his reach" (4T 569).

"Stand like Daniel, that faithful statesman, a man whom no temptation could corrupt" (COL 332 [see also GC 470; OHC 249]).

Are there people living above sin today?

"In every phase of your character building you are to please God. This you may do; for Enoch pleased Him though living in a degenerate age. And there are Enochs in this our day" (COL 332).

Do those Christians who are living the closest to Christ realize how saintly they are?

"The closer you come to Jesus, the more faulty you will appear in your own eyes; for your vision will be clearer, and your imperfections will be seen in broad and distinct contrast to His perfect nature. This is evidence that Satan's delusions have lost their power; that the vivifying influence of the Spirit of God is arousing you" (SC 64, 65).

"The more we contemplate the character of Christ, and the more we experience of His saving power, the more keenly shall we realize our own weakness and imperfection, and the more earnestly shall we look to Him as our strength and our Redeemer" (SL 83).

"The nearer we come to Jesus, and the more clearly we discern the purity of His character, the more clearly shall we see the exceeding sinfulness of sin, and the less shall we feel like exalting ourselves. There will be a continual reaching out of the soul after God, a continual, earnest, heartbreaking confession of sin and humbling of the heart before Him. At every advance step in our Christian experience our repentance will deepen" (AA 561).

"Those who experience the sanctification of the Bible

147

will manifest a spirit of humility. Like Moses, they have had a view of the awful majesty of holiness, and they see their own unworthiness in contrast with the purity and exalted perfection of the Infinite One" (GC 470).

"Those who are really seeking to perfect Christian character will never indulge the thought that they are sinless" (SL 7).

"The greater the distance between them and their Saviour, the more righteous they appear in their own eyes" (SL 8).

"No one who claims holiness is really holy. Those who are registered as holy in the books of heaven are not aware of the fact, and are the last ones to boast of their own goodness" (ST Feb. 26, 1885).

What is Christ's attitude toward those who commit sin while sincerely trying to be Christians?

"We shall often have to bow down and weep at the feet of Jesus because of our shortcomings and mistakes, but we are not to be discouraged. Even if we are overcome by the enemy, we are not cast off, not forsaken and rejected of God" (SC 64).

"Jesus loves His children, even if they err. . . . When they do their best, calling upon God for His help, be assured the service will be accepted, although imperfect. Jesus is perfect. Christ's righteousness is imputed unto them, and He will say, 'Take away the filthy garments from him and clothe him with change of raiment.' Jesus makes up for our unavoidable deficiencies" (18MR 244).

"When it is in the heart to obey God, when efforts are put forth to this end, Jesus accepts this disposition and effort as man's best service, and He makes up for the deficiency with His own divine merit" (1SM 382 [ML 250]).

"If one who daily communes with God errs from the

path, if he turns a moment from looking steadfastly unto Jesus, it is not because he sins willfully; for when he sees his mistake, he turns again, and fastens his eyes upon Jesus, and the fact that he has erred, does not make him less dear to the heart of God" (FL 118 [RH May 12, 1896]).

"If through manifold temptations we are surprised or deceived into sin, He does not turn from us and leave us to perish. No, no, that is not our Saviour. . . . Our faith looks up to Him, grasps Him as the One who can save to the uttermost, and the fragrance of the all-sufficient offering is accepted of the Father" (OHC 49).

"When, through faith in Jesus Christ, man does according to the very best of his ability, and seeks to keep the way of the Lord by obedience to the ten commandments, the perfection of Christ is imputed to cover the transgression of the repentant and obedient soul" (FE 135).

What should the Christian's attitude be when he or she falls into sin?

"If you make failures and are betrayed into sin, do not feel then you cannot pray . . . but seek the Lord more earnestly" (OHC 49).

"When we are clothed with the righteousness of Christ, we shall have no relish for sin; for Christ will be working with us. We may make mistakes, but we will hate the sin that caused the sufferings of the Son of God" (1SM 360 [MYP 338]).

"Do all in your power to gain perfection; but do not think that because you make mistakes you are excluded from God's service" (MYP 226).

"When Satan tells you that the Lord will not regard you with favor because you have sinned, say, 'Jesus gave His life for me. He suffered a cruel death that He might enable me to resist temptation. I know that He loves me, notwithstanding my imperfection. I rest in His love. God has accepted His perfection in my behalf. He is my righteousness, and I trust in His merits'" (ST Aug. 13, 1902).

Does the pen of inspiration tell us of other God-fearing persons who also at times were overcome by temptations?

"The pen of inspiration, true to its task, tells us of the sins that overcame Noah, Lot, Moses, Abraham, David, and Solomon, and that even Elijah's strong spirit sank under temptation during his fearful trial. Jonah's disobedience and Israel's idolatry are faithfully recorded. Peter's denial of Christ, the sharp contention of Paul and Barnabas, the failings and infirmities of the prophets and apostles, are all laid bare by the Holy Ghost, who lifts the veil from the human heart. There before us lie the lives of the believers, with all their faults and follies, which are intended as a lesson to all the generations following them. If they had been without foible they would have been more than human, and our sinful natures would despair of ever reaching such a point of excellence. But seeing where they struggled and fell, where they took heart again and conquered through the grace of God, we are encouraged, and led to press over the obstacles that degenerate nature places in our way" (4T 12).

What is the difference between the Christian who sometimes is led into sin and the worldling who commits the same sin?

"While the followers of Christ have sinned, they have not given themselves to the control of evil" (5T 474).

"To be led into sin unawares—not intending to sin, but to sin through want of watchfulness and prayer, not discerning the temptation of Satan and so falling into his snare—is very different from the one who plans and deliberately enters into temptation and plans out a course of sin" (OHC 177).

"The character is revealed, not by occasional good deeds and occasional misdeeds, but by the tendency of the habitual words and acts" (SC 57, 58).

Is there any difference between the professed Christian who is a slave to just one bad habit, and the worldling?

"One sinful desire cherished will eventually neutralize all the power of the gospel" (5T 53).

"One secret sin indulged will prove to the character what the worm-eaten plank does to the ship—utter disaster and ruin" (4T 90).

"One defect, cultivated instead of being overcome, makes the man imperfect, and closes against him the gate of the Holy City" (MYP 144).

What great blessing of heaven will soon be poured out on those who have gained the victory over every besetting sin and who are not controlled by evil?

(See page 94, "Cleanse soul temple of every defilement.")

"Those who would rather die than perform a wrong act are the only ones who will be found faithful" (5T 53 [see also SC 38]).

What is the purpose of the latter rain?

"The latter rain, falling near the close of the season, ripens the grain, and prepares it for the sickle. The Lord employs these operations of nature to represent the work of the Holy Spirit. . . . The ripening of the grain represents the completion of the work of God's grace in the soul. By the power of the Holy Spirit the moral image of God is to be perfected in the character. We are to be wholly transformed into the likeness of Christ. The latter rain, ripening earth's harvest, represents the spiritual grace that prepares the church for the coming of the Son of man" (TM 506).

"As we seek God for the Holy Spirit, it will work in us meekness, humbleness of mind, a conscious dependence upon God for the perfecting latter rain" (*ibid.* 509).

Under the power of the perfecting latter rain, to what spiritual state will God's people—the 144,000—be brought by the close of probation?

Rev. 14:1, 5.

"Are we seeking for His fullness, ever pressing toward the mark set before us—the perfection of His character? When the Lord's people reach this mark, they will be sealed in their foreheads. Filled with the Spirit, they will be complete in Christ, and the recording angel will declare, 'It is finished'" (OHC 150).

Is a long period of years necessarily required for the perfection of Christian character?

"As we near the close of this earth's history, we either rapidly advance in Christian growth, or we rapidly retrograde toward the world" (RH Dec. 13, 1892).

"What we have been years learning, they will have to learn in a few months" (EW 67).

Why is it absolutely necessary for the 144,000 not to sin even by a thought after the close of probation?

"They have passed through the time of trouble such as never was since there was a nation; . . . they have stood without an intercessor through the final outpouring of God's judgments" (GC 649).

Will they still feel the promptings of sin and be tempted after probation has closed?

"So long as Satan reigns, we shall have self to subdue, besetting sins to overcome; so long as life shall last, there will be no stopping place, no point which we can reach and say, I have fully attained. Sanctification is the result of lifelong obedience" (AA 560, 561 [see also 1T 341]).

"To those who have tried so hard to obtain by faith so-called holy flesh, I would say, You cannot obtain it. Not a soul of you has holy flesh now. No human being on earth has holy flesh. . . . We may have Christian perfection of the soul. Through the sacrifice made in our behalf, sins may be perfectly forgiven. . . . Thank God that we are not dealing with impossibilities. We may claim sanctification" (2SM 32).

"We may create an unreal world in our own mind and picture an ideal church, where the temptations of Satan no longer prompt to evil; but perfection exists only in our imagination" (RH Aug. 8, 1893).

When will all temptation cease?

"When human beings receive holy flesh, they will not remain on the earth, but will be taken to heaven. While sin is forgiven in this life, its results are not now wholly removed. It is at His coming that Christ is to 'change our vile body, that it may be fashioned like unto his glorious body' (Phil. 3:21)" (2SM 33).

"I heard shouts of triumph from the angels and from the redeemed saints which sounded like ten thousand musical instruments, because they were to be no more annoyed and tempted by Satan and because the inhabitants of other worlds were delivered from his presence and his temptations" (SR 416).

"There are hereditary and cultivated tendencies to evil

that must be overcome. Appetite and passion must be brought under the control of the Holy Spirit. There is no end to the warfare this side of eternity" (CT 20).

THE
DEATH DECREE

What is Satan's ultimate intention concerning God's people?

Rev. 13:15.

"The remnant church will be brought into great trial and distress. Those who keep the commandments of God and the faith of Jesus will feel the ire of the dragon and his hosts. Satan numbers the world as his subjects, he has gained control of the apostate churches; but here is a little company that are resisting his supremacy. If he could blot them from the earth, his triumph would be complete. As he influenced the heathen nations to destroy Israel, so in the near future he will stir up the wicked powers of earth to destroy the people of God" (9T 231).

How will Satan attempt to accomplish his purpose?

"Says the great deceiver: '. . . Our principal concern is to silence this sect of Sabbathkeepers. We must excite popular indignation against them. We will enlist great men and worldly-wise men upon our side, and induce those in authority to carry out our purposes. Then the sabbath which I have set up shall be enforced by laws the most severe and exacting. Those who disregard them shall be driven out from the cities and villages, and made to suffer hunger and privation. When once we have the power, we will show what we can do with those who will not swerve from their allegiance to God. We led the Romish church to inflict imprisonment, torture, and death upon those who refused to yield to her decrees; and now that we are bringing the Protestant churches and the world into harmony with this right arm of our strength, we will finally have a law to exterminate all who will not submit to our authority. When death shall be made the penalty of violating our sabbath, then many who are now ranked with commandment keepers will come over to our side' " (TM 472, 473).

Will death be included, at first, as the penalty for violating the universal Sunday law?

"The powers of earth, uniting to war against the commandments of God, will decree that 'all, both small and great, rich and poor, free and bond' (Rev. 13:16), shall conform to the customs of the church by the observance of the false sabbath. All who refuse compliance will be visited with civil penalties, and it will finally be declared that they are deserving of death" (GC 604).

When, in relationship to the close of probation, will capital punishment become the penalty for breaking the Sunday law?

"Wonderful events are soon to open before the world. The end of all things is at hand. The time of trouble is about to come upon the people of God. Then it is that the decree will go forth forbidding those who keep the Sabbath of the Lord to buy or sell, and threatening them with punishment, and even death, if they do not observe the first day of the week as the Sabbath. 'And at that time shall Michael stand up, the great prince which standeth for the children of thy people: and there shall be a time of trouble, such as never was since there was a nation even to that same time'" (RH Nov. 19, 1908).

" 'And at that time shall Michael stand up, the great prince which standeth for the children of thy people: and there shall be a time of trouble, such as never was since there was a nation even to that same time: and at that time thy people shall be delivered, everyone that shall be found written in the book.' When this time of trouble comes, every case is decided; there is no longer probation, no longer mercy for the impenitent. The seal of the living God is upon His people. This small remnant, unable to defend themselves in the deadly conflict with the powers of earth that are marshaled by the dragon host, make God their defense. The decree has been passed by the highest earthly authority that they shall worship the beast and receive his mark under pain of persecution and death. May God help His people now, for what can they then do in such a fearful conflict without His assistance!" (5T 212, 213).

When Adventist are threatened with imprisonment and death, will some give up their faith?

"The time is not far distant when the test will come to every soul. The mark of the beast will be urged upon us. Those who have step by step yielded to worldly demands and conformed to worldly customs will not find it a hard matter to yield to the powers that be, rather than subject themselves to derision, insult, threatened imprisonment, and death. The contest is between the commandments of God and the commandments of men. In this time the gold will be separated from the dross in the church" (*ibid.* 81).

Will there be some martyrdoms?

"As he influenced the heathen nations to destroy Israel, so in the near future he will stir up the wicked powers of earth to destroy the people of God. Men will be required to render obedience to human edicts in violation of the divine law. Those who are true to God will be menaced, denounced, proscribed. They will be 'betrayed both by parents, and brethren, and kinsfolk, and friends,' even unto death" (PK 587, 588).

In this hour of deepest apostasy, will there be Adventists in every land who will prove true?

"In heathen Africa, in the Catholic lands of Europe and of South America, in China, in India, in the islands of the sea, and in all the dark corners of the earth, God has in reserve a firmament of chosen ones that will yet shine forth amidst the darkness, revealing clearly to an apostate world the transforming power of obedience to His law. Even now they are appearing in every nation, among every tongue and people; and in the hour of deepest apostasy, when Satan's supreme effort is made to cause 'all, both small and great, rich and poor, free and bond,' to receive, under penalty of death, the sign of allegiance to a false rest day, these faithful ones, 'blameless and harmless, the sons of God, without rebuke,' will 'shine as lights in the world' (Rev. 13:16; Phil. 2:15)" (PK 188, 189).

When probation closes and the plagues begin to fall, who will be blamed as the cause of these judgments?

"These plagues enraged the wicked against the righteous; they thought that we had brought the judgments of God upon them, and that if they could rid the earth of us, the plagues would then be stayed" (EW 36).

What will be the result of this reasoning?

"It will be urged that the few who stand in opposition to an institution of the church and a law of the state ought not to be tolerated; that it is better for them to suffer than for whole nations to be thrown into confusion and lawlessness. The same argument eighteen hundred years ago was brought against Christ by the 'rulers of the people.' . . . This argument will appear conclusive; and a decree will finally be issued against those who hallow the Sabbath of the fourth commandment, denouncing them as deserving of the severest punishment and giving the people liberty, after a certain time, to put them to death" (GC 615).

"I saw the leading men of the earth consulting together, and Satan and his angels busy around them. I saw a writing, copies of which were scattered in different parts of the land, giving orders that unless the saints should yield their peculiar faith, give up the Sabbath, and observe the first day of the week, the people were at liberty after a certain time to put them to death" (EW 282, 283 [SR 406]).

"When Jesus leaves the most holy, His restraining Spirit is withdrawn from rulers and people. They are left to the control of evil angels. Then such laws will be made by the counsel and direction of Satan, that unless time should be very short, no flesh could be saved" (1T 204).

"Especially will the wrath of man be aroused against those who hallow the Sabbath of the fourth commandment; and at last a universal decree will denounce these as deserving of death" (PK 512).

What terrible time of trouble for the righteous will follow the issuing of the universal death decree?

"A decree went forth to slay the saints, which caused them to cry day and night for deliverance. This was the time of Jacob's trouble" (EW 36, 37).

See other quotations on pages 170 and 171 under the questions "What will be the immediate cause of this terrible period of distress?" and "Why is this crisis called 'the time of Jacob's trouble'?"

Will there be a specific date set by this decree after which Seventh-day Adventists may be killed?

"Though a general decree has fixed the time when commandment-keepers may be put to death, their enemies will in some cases anticipate the decree, and before the time specified, will endeavor to take their lives" (GC 631).

What ancient decree also had a date set for the destruction of God's people?

"The decree which is to go forth against the people of God will be very similar to that issued by Ahasuerus against the Jews in the time of Esther" (5T 450 [see also PK 605; Esther 3:12, 13]).

Which plague follows the universal death decree?

"And 'the rivers and fountains of waters . . . became blood.' Terrible as these inflictions are, God's justice stands fully vindicated. The angel of God declares: 'Thou art righteous, O Lord, . . . because thou hast judged thus. For they have shed the blood of saints and prophets, and thou hast given them blood to drink; for they are worthy (Rev. 16: 2-6).' By condemning the people of God to death, they have as truly incurred the guilt of their blood as if it had been shed by their hands" (GC 628).

While they are waiting to be slain, where will God's people be?

"As the decree issued by the various rulers of Christendom against commandment keepers shall withdraw the protection of government and abandon them to those who desire their destruction, the people of God will flee from the cities and villages and associate together in companies, dwelling in the most desolate and solitary places. Many will find refuge in the strongholds of the mountains. . . . But many of all nations, and of all classes, high and low, rich and poor, black and white, will be cast into the most unjust and cruel bondage. The beloved of God pass weary days, bound in chains, shut in by prison bars, sentenced to be slain, some apparently left to die of starvation in dark and loathsome dungeons" (ibid. 626).

"The people of God—some in prison cells, some hidden in solitary retreats in the forests and the mountains—still plead for divine protection, while in every quarter companies of armed men, urged on by hosts of evil angels, are preparing for the work of death" (ibid. 635).

"The people of God are not at this time all in one place. They are in different companies, and in all parts of the earth; and they will be tried singly, not in groups. Every one must stand the test for himself" (4BC 1143).

What will the wicked try to do to the righteous who have remained in the cities and villages?

"As the saints left the cities and villages, they were pursued by the wicked, who sought to slay them. But the swords that were raised to kill God's people broke and fell as powerless as a straw. Angels of God shielded the saints" (EW 284, 285).

"In the time of trouble we all fled from the cities and villages, but were pursued by the wicked, who entered the houses of the saints with a sword. They raised the sword to kill us, but it broke, and fell as powerless as a straw" (EW 34).

As the death decree approaches, what do some of the saints fear?

"Some began to fear that God had at last left them to perish by the hand of the wicked" (EW 283).

"Yet to human sight it will appear that the people of

God must soon seal their testimony with their blood as did the martyrs before them. They themselves begin to fear that the Lord has left them to fall by the hand of their enemies. It is a time of fearful agony. Day and night they cry unto God for deliverance. The wicked exult, and the jeering cry is heard: 'Where now is your faith? Why does not God deliver you out of our hands if you are indeed His people?' But the waiting ones remember Jesus dying upon Calvary's cross and the chief priests and rulers shouting in mockery: 'He saved others; himself he cannot save. If he be the King of Israel, let him now come down from the cross, and we will believe him (Matt. 27:42).' Like Jacob, all are wrestling with God. Their countenances express their internal struggle. Paleness sits on every face. Yet they cease not their earnest intercession" (GC 630).

"The eye of God, looking down the ages, was fixed upon the crisis which His people are to meet, when earthly powers shall be arrayed against them. Like the captive exile, they will be in fear of death by starvation or by violence" (*ibid.* 634).

What three separate groups of beings surround the saints at this time?

"But if their eyes could have been opened, they would have seen themselves surrounded by angels of God. Next came the multitude of the angry wicked, and next a mass of evil angels, hurrying on the wicked to slay the saints. But before they would approach God's people, the wicked must first pass this company of mighty, holy angels. This was impossible" (EW 283 [see also 9T 17]).

How will the wicked plan to destroy God's people?

"When the protection of human laws shall be withdrawn from those who honor the law of God, there will be, in different lands, a simultaneous movement for their destruction. As the time appointed in the decree draws near, the people will conspire to root out the hated sect. It will be determined to strike in one night a decisive blow, which shall utterly silence the voice of dissent and reproof" (GC 635).

How will God deliver His faithful children?

"With shouts of triumph, jeering, and imprecation, throngs of evil men are about to rush upon their prey, when, lo, a dense blackness, deeper than the darkness of the night, falls upon the earth. . . . It is at midnight that God manifests His power for the deliverance of His people. . . . The proudest cities of the earth are laid low. The lordly palaces, upon which the world's great men have lavished their wealth in order to glorify themselves, are crumbling to ruin before their eyes. Prison walls are rent asunder, and God's people, who have been held in bondage for their faith, are set free" (*ibid.* 635-637).

"I saw that God will in a wonderful manner preserve His people through the time of trouble. As Jesus poured out His soul in agony in the garden, they will earnestly cry and agonize day and night for deliverance. The decree will go forth that they must disregard the Sabbath of the fourth commandment, and honor the first day, or lose their lives; but they will not yield, and trample under their feet the Sabbath of the Lord, and honor an institution of papacy. Satan's host and wicked men will surround them, and exult over them, because there will seem to be no way of escape for them. But in the midst of their revelry and triumph, there is heard peal upon peal of the loudest thunder. The heavens have gathered blackness, and are only illuminated by the blazing light

163

and terrible glory from heaven, as God utters His voice from His holy habitation.

"The foundations of the earth shake; buildings totter and fall with a terrible crash. The sea boils like a pot, and the whole earth is in terrible commotion. The captivity of the righteous is turned, and with sweet and solemn whisperings they say to one another: 'We are delivered. It is the voice of God'" (1T 353, 354).

"The darkest hour of the church's struggle with the powers of evil is that which immediately precedes the day of her final deliverance" (PK 725).

How many of the saints will be slain under this death decree?

"God would not suffer the wicked to destroy those who were expecting translation and who would not bow to the decree of the beast or receive his mark. I saw that if the wicked were permitted to slay the saints, Satan and all his evil host, and all who hate God, would be gratified. And oh, what a triumph it would be for his satanic majesty to have power, in the last closing struggle, over those who had so long waited to behold Him whom they loved! Those who have mocked at the idea of the saints' going up will witness the care of God for His people and behold their glorious deliverance" (EW 284).

"If the blood of Christ's faithful witnesses were shed at this time, it would not, like the blood of the martyrs, be as seed sown to yield a harvest for God. . . . Glorious will be the deliverance of those who have patiently waited for His coming and whose names are written in the book of life" (GC 634).

What event will climax all of history?

"Soon there appears in the east a small black cloud,

about half the size of a man's hand. . . . The King of kings descends upon the cloud, wrapped in flaming fire" (*ibid.* 640, 641).

THE TIME OF JACOB'S TROUBLE

How did the Lord describe the dreadful period of anguish that the king of Babylon would bring upon Judah?

Jer. 30:5-7.

Shortly after the angel of mercy takes her flight, what will Satan and his hosts bring upon modern Israel?

"As the approach of the Roman armies was a sign to the disciples of the impending destruction of Jerusalem, so may this apostasy be a sign to us that the limit of God's forbearance is reached, that the measure of our nation's iniquity is full, and that the angel of mercy is about to take her flight, never to return. The people of God will then be plunged into those scenes of affliction and distress which prophets have described as the time of Jacob's trouble" (5T 451).

Over what issue will Satan stir up all the world against Seventh-day Adventists?

"As the Sabbath has become the special point of controversy throughout Christendom, and religious and secular authorities have combined to enforce the observance of the Sunday, the persistent refusal of a small minority to yield to the popular demand will make them objects of universal execration" (GC 615).

What will be the immediate cause of this terrible period of distress?

"I saw that the four angels would hold the four winds

until Jesus' work was done in the sanctuary, and then will come the seven last plagues. These plagues enraged the wicked against the righteous; they thought that we had brought the judgments of God upon them, and that if they could rid the earth of us, the plagues would then be stayed. A decree went forth to slay the saints, which caused them to cry day and night for deliverance. This was the time of Jacob's trouble" (EW 36, 37).

"A decree will finally be issued against those who hallow the Sabbath of the fourth commandment, denouncing them as deserving of the severest punishment and giving the people liberty, after a certain time, to put them to death. Romanism in the Old World and apostate Protestantism in the New will pursue a similar course toward those who honor all the divine precepts.

"The people of God will then be plunged into those scenes of affliction and distress described by the prophet as the time of Jacob's trouble" (GC 615, 616).

Why is this crisis called "the time of Jacob's trouble"?
Gen. 32:24-28.

"Jacob and Esau represent two classes: Jacob, the righteous, and Esau, the wicked. Jacob's distress when he learned that Esau was marching against him with four hundred men represents the trouble of the righteous as the decree goes forth to put them to death, just before the coming of the Lord. As the wicked gather about them, they will be filled with anguish, for, like Jacob, they can see no escape for their lives. The angel placed himself before Jacob, and he took hold of the angel and held him and wrestled with him all night. So also will the righteous, in their time of trouble and anguish, wrestle in prayer with God, as Jacob wrestled with the angel. Jacob in his distress prayed all night for deliverance from the hand of Esau. The

167

righteous in their mental anguish will cry to God day and night for deliverance from the hand of the wicked who surround them" (SR 97 [3SG 131, 132]).

"Jacob's experience during that night of wrestling and anguish represents the trial through which the people of God must pass just before Christ's second coming. The prophet Jeremiah, in holy vision looking down to this time, said, '. . . Alas! for that day is great, so that none is like it: it is even the time of Jacob's trouble; but he shall be saved out of it' (Jer. 30:5-7).

"When Christ shall cease His work as mediator in man's behalf, then this time of trouble will begin. Then the case of every soul will have been decided, and there will be no atoning blood to cleanse from sin. When Jesus leaves His position as man's intercessor before God, the solemn announcement is made, 'He that is unjust, let him be unjust still . . .' (Rev. 22:11). Then the restraining Spirit of God is withdrawn from the earth. As Jacob was threatened with death by his angry brother, so the people of God will be in peril from the wicked who are seeking to destroy them. And as the patriarch wrestled all night for deliverance from the hand of Esau, so the righteous will cry to God day and night for deliverance from the enemies that surround them" (PP 201).

Do all Seventh-day Adventists agree that the "time of Jacob's trouble" will begin with the universal death decree after probation's close?

No, they do not. There are some who believe that the time of Jacob's trouble will begin with the national Sunday law prior to the close of probation. Their conclusion is based on the following statement:

"To secure popularity and patronage, legislators will yield to the demand for a Sunday law. . . . As the approach of the Roman armies was a sign to the disciples of the impending destruction of Jerusalem, so may this apostasy be a sign to us that the limit of God's forbearance is reached, that the measure of our nation's iniquity is full, and that the angel of mercy is about to take her flight, never to return. The people of God will then be plunged into those scenes of affliction and distress which prophets have described as the time of Jacob's trouble" (5T 451).

Actually, the statement in 5T 451 harmonizes perfectly with quotations already cited. The people of God will "then" (after the angel of mercy takes her flight) be plunged into the time of Jacob's trouble.

Can we get a complete picture of this bitter ordeal from the Spirit of Prophecy?

"The 'time of trouble, such as never was' is soon to open upon us; and we shall need an experience which we do not now possess and which many are too indolent to obtain. It is often the case that trouble is greater in anticipation than in reality; but this is not true of the crisis before us. The most vivid presentation cannot reach the magnitude of the ordeal. In that time of trial, every soul must stand for himself before God" (GC 622).

Would the time of Jacob's trouble be too severe a test for even some genuine Christians?

1 Cor. 10:13.

"It is not always safe to ask for unconditional healing. . . . He knows whether or not those for whom petitions are offered would be able to endure the trial and test that would come upon them if they lived. He knows the end from the beginning. Many will be laid away to sleep before the fiery ordeal of the time of trouble shall come upon our world" (CH 375).

"The Lord has often instructed me that many little ones are to be laid away before the time of trouble. We shall see our children again. We shall meet them and know them in the heavenly courts" (2SM 259).

Where will the people of God be at this time?

See quotations on page 165, "While they are waiting to be slain, where will God's people be?"

Is it advisable for us to plan now for our temporal wants in the time of trouble?

"The Lord has shown me repeatedly that it is contrary to the Bible to make any provision for our temporal wants in the time of trouble. I saw that if the saints had food laid up by them or in the field in the time of trouble, when sword, famine, and pestilence are in the land, it would be taken from them by violent hands and strangers would reap their fields" (EW 56).

"Houses and lands will be of no use to the saints in the time of trouble, for they will then have to flee before infuriated mobs" (*ibid.* 56).

Who will sustain us?

"Then will be the time for us to trust wholly in God, and He will sustain us" (*ibid.* 56).

"In the time of trouble, just previous to the coming of Christ, the lives of the righteous will be preserved through the ministration of holy angels" (ST Feb. 26, 1880).

"That God who cared for Elijah will not pass by one of His self-sacrificing children. He who numbers the hairs of their head will care for them, and in time of famine they shall be satisfied. While the wicked are dying from hunger and pestilence, angels will shield the righteous and supply their wants. To him that 'walketh righteously' is the promise: 'Bread shall be given him; his waters shall be sure' (Isa. 33:15, 16)" (GC 629).

How much food will the saints be provided?

"The time of trouble is just before us; and then stern necessity will require the people of God to deny self, and to eat merely enough to sustain life; but God will prepare us for that time. In that fearful hour our necessity will be God's opportunity to impart His strengthening power, and to sustain His people" (1T 206 [CD 202]).

"Bread and water is all that is promised to the remnant in the time of trouble" (3SG 252 [SR 129]).

"The people of God will not be free from suffering; but while persecuted and distressed, while they endure privation and suffer for want of food they will not be left to perish" (GC 629).

"Angels provided them food and water, while the wicked were suffering from hunger and thirst" (EW 282).

"I saw that our bread and water will be sure at that time, and that we shall not lack or suffer hunger; for God is able to spread a table for us in the wilderness. If necessary He would send ravens to feed us, as He did to feed Elijah, or rain manna from heaven, as He did for the Israelites" (*ibid.* 56).

"Certain destruction threatens them, and like Jacob they will not suffer their faith to grow weak, because their prayers are not immediately answered. Though suffering the pangs of hunger, they will not cease their intercessions" (3SG 135).

How much moral support can we count on from our friends during this trying ordeal?

"The faith of individual members of the church will be tested as though there were not another person in the world" (7BC 983).

Will the Lord immediately answer the prayers of His people when they call upon Him for deliverance?

"The very delay, so painful to them, is the best answer to their petitions. As they endeavor to wait trustingly for the Lord to work they are led to exercise faith, hope, and patience, which have been too little exercised during their religious experience" (GC 631).

"The season of distress and anguish before us will require a faith that can endure weariness, delay, and hunger— a faith that will not faint though severely tried" (*ibid.* 621).

What will some of the saints begin to fear?

See quotations on page 166.

In spite of persecution and hunger, what is really the chief cause of their anguish?

"Though God's people will be surrounded by enemies who are bent upon their destruction, yet the anguish which they suffer is not a dread of persecution for the truth's sake; they fear that every sin has not been repented of, and that through some fault in themselves they will fail to realize the fulfillment of the Saviour's promise: I 'will keep thee from the hour of temptation, which shall come upon all the world' (Rev. 3:10). If they could have the assurance of pardon they would not shrink from torture or death; but should they prove unworthy, and lose their lives because of their own defects of character, then God's holy name would be reproached" (*ibid.* 619).

What opinion do they have of themselves?

"The righteous, in their distress, will have a deep sense of their unworthiness, and with many tears will acknowledge their utter unworthiness, and like Jacob will plead the promises of God through Christ, made to just such dependent, helpless, repenting sinners" (3SG 132 [SR 97; 1SP 121, 122]).

Will the saints, of themselves, be able to recall any particular sins that they have committed?

"They cannot bring to mind any particular sins, but in their whole life they can see but little good. Their sins had gone beforehand to judgment, and pardon had been written. Their sins had been borne away into the land of forgetfulness, and they could not bring them to remembrance" (3SG 135 [1SP 124]).

"But while they have a deep sense of their unworthiness, they have no concealed wrongs to reveal. Their sins have gone beforehand to judgment and have been blotted out, and they cannot bring them to remembrance" (GC 620).

However, when the righteous are reminded of their past sins, into what depths of near despair will they be driven?

"Jacob took firm hold of the angel in his distress and would not let him go. As he made supplication with tears, the angel reminded him of his past wrongs and endeavored to escape from Jacob, to test him and prove him. So will the righteous, in the day of their anguish, be tested, proved, and tried, to manifest their strength of faith, their perseverance and unshaken confidence in the power of God to deliver them.

"Jacob would not be turned away, He knew that God was merciful, and he appealed to His mercy. He pointed back to his past sorrow for, and repentance of, his wrongs, and urged his petition for deliverance from the hand of Esau. Thus his importuning continued all night. As he reviewed his past wrongs he was driven almost to despair. But he knew that he must have help from God, or perish.

He held the angel fast and urged his petition with agonizing, earnest cries, until he prevailed. Thus will it be with the righteous. As they review the events of their past life, their hopes will almost sink" (SR 97, 98 [3SG 132, 133]).

"As Satan accuses the people of God on account of their sins, the Lord permits him to try them to the uttermost. Their confidence in God, their faith and firmness, will be severely tested. As they review the past, their hopes sink; for in their whole lives they can see little good" (GC 618, 619).

What appeal will the righteous make to God concerning their many sins?

"But as they realize that it is a case of life or death, they will earnestly cry unto God, and appeal to Him in regard to their past sorrow and humble repentance of their many sins, and then will refer to His promise, 'Let him take hold of my strength, and make peace with me, and he shall make peace with me.' Thus will their earnest petitions be offered to God day and night" (3SG 133).

"They afflict their souls before God, pointing to their past repentance of their many sins" (GC 619).

How many unconfessed sins are brought to their remembrance?

"They will feel their unworthiness, but will have no concealed wrongs to reveal. If they had sins, unconfessed and unrepented of, to appear then before them, while tortured with fear and anguish, with a lively sense of all their unworthiness, they would be overwhelmed" (3SG 134 [SR 98]).

"So, in the time of trouble, if the people of God had unconfessed sins to appear before them while tortured with fear and anguish, they would be overwhelmed; despair would cut off their faith, and they could not have confidence to plead with God for deliverance. But while they have a deep sense of their unworthiness, they have no concealed wrongs to reveal" (GC 620).

What variations will be found in the anguish of the saints?

"Those who exercise but little faith now are in the greatest danger of falling under the power of satanic delusions and the decree to compel the conscience. And even if they endure the test they will be plunged into deeper distress and anguish in the time of trouble, because they have never made it a habit to trust in God" (*ibid.* 622).

How will the Lord answer the prayers of His people, even before they are delivered from their enemies?

"Though enemies may thrust them into prison, yet dungeon walls cannot cut off the communication between their souls and Christ. One who sees their every weakness, who is acquainted with every trial, is above all earthly powers; and angels will come to them in lonely cells, bringing light and peace from heaven. The prison will be as a palace; for the rich in faith dwell there, and the gloomy walls will be lighted up with heavenly light, as when Paul and Silas prayed and sang praises at midnight in the Philippian dungeon" (GC 627 [see also PK 512, 513]).

"As the wrestling ones urge their petitions before God, the veil separating them from the unseen seems almost withdrawn. The heavens glow with the dawning of eternal day, and like the melody of angel songs the words fall upon the ear, 'Stand fast to your allegiance. Help is coming.' . . . The precious Saviour will send help just when we need it" (GC 632, 633).

"Could men see with heavenly vision, they would behold companies of angels that excel in strength stationed about those who have kept the word of Christ's patience.

With sympathizing tenderness, angels have witnessed their distress and have heard their prayers. They are waiting the word of their Commander to snatch them from their peril" (*ibid.* 630).

How will the Lord finally bring deliverance to His people?

"With shouts of triumph, jeering, and imprecation, throngs of evil men are about to rush upon their prey, when, lo, a dense blackness, deeper than the darkness of the night, falls upon the earth. . . . It is at midnight that God manifests His power for the deliverance of His people. . . . In the midst of the angry heavens is one clear space of indescribable glory, whence comes the voice of God like the sound of many waters, saying, 'It is done' (Rev. 16:17)" (*ibid.* 635, 636).

See quotations on page 167, "How will God deliver His faithful children?"

What is the number of those who will victoriously pass through the time of Jacob's trouble?

Rev. 7:4; 14:1.

How will their experience differ from that of any other group of Christians since time began?

"And they sing 'a new song' before the throne, a song which no man can learn save the hundred and forty and four thousand. It is the song of Moses and the Lamb—a song of deliverance. None but the hundred and forty-four thousand can learn that song; for it is the song of their experience—an experience such as no other company have ever had. 'These are they which follow the Lamb whithersoever he goeth.' These, having been translated from the earth, from among the living, are counted as 'the firstfruits unto God and to the Lamb (Rev. 14:1-5).' 'These are they which came out of great tribulation

176

(Rev. 7:14-17);' they have passed through the time of trouble such as never was since there was a nation; they have endured the anguish of the time of Jacob's trouble; they have stood without an intercessor through the final outpouring of God's judgments" (*ibid.* 648, 649).

How many sins will they commit during the entire period of the great time of trouble—from the close of probation until the coming of Jesus in the clouds?

"Not even by a thought could our Saviour be brought to yield to the power of temptation. . . . This is the condition in which those must be found who shall stand in the time of trouble" (*ibid.* 623).

For whose benefit has this marvelous exhibit of sinlessness been demonstrated?

"In sparing the life of the first murderer, God presented before the whole universe a lesson bearing upon the great controversy. . . .

"It was His purpose, not merely to put down the rebellion, but to demonstrate to all the universe the nature of the rebellion. . . . The holy inhabitants of other worlds were watching with the deepest interest the events taking place on the earth. . . .

"God carries with Him the sympathy and approval of the whole universe as step by step His great plan advances to its complete fulfillment" (PP 78, 79).

"But the plan of redemption had a yet broader and deeper purpose than the salvation of man. It was not for this alone that Christ came to the earth; it was not merely that the inhabitants of this little world might regard the law of God as it should be regarded; but it was to vindicate the character of God before the universe. To this result of His great sacrifice—its influence upon the intelligences of other worlds, as well as upon man—the Saviour looked forward when just before His crucifixion He said, 'Now is the judgment of this world: now shall the prince of this world be cast out. And I, if I be lifted up from the earth, will draw all men unto Me' (John 12:31, 32). The act of Christ in dying for the salvation of man would not only make heaven accessible to men, but before all the universe it would justify God and His Son in their dealing with the rebellion of Satan" (*ibid.* 68, 69).

"The worlds unfallen and the heavenly angels had watched with intense interest as the conflict drew to its close" (DA 693).

"We are like men condemned to death in the arena, a spectacle to the whole universe—angels as well as men" (1 Cor. 4:9, NEB).

"The whole universe is watching with inexpressible interest the closing scenes of the great controversy between good and evil" (PK 148).

"Our little world is the lesson book of the universe" (DA 19).

THE GREAT TIME OF TROUBLE

(After Probation's Close)

Who today is keeping the forces of destruction from sweeping over our earth?

Rev. 7:1-3.

"Angels are belting the world, refusing Satan his claims to supremacy, made because of the vast multitude of his adherents. We hear not the voices, we see not with the natural sight the work of these angels, but their hands are linked about the world, and with sleepless vigilance they are keeping the armies of Satan at bay till the sealing of God's people shall be accomplished" (7BC 967).

"John sees the elements of nature—earthquakes, tempest, and political strife—represented as being held by four angels. These winds are under control until God gives the word to let them go" (TM 444).

"The same destructive power exercised by holy angels when God commands will be exercised by evil angels when He permits. There are forces now ready, and only waiting the divine permission, to spread desolation everywhere" (GC 614).

What is the last act in the drama, after which probation will be closed and Satan will be allowed to work his will on the earth?

"This earth has almost reached the place where God will permit the destroyer to work his will upon it. The substitution of the laws of men for the law of God, the exaltation, by merely human authority, of Sunday in place of the

Bible Sabbath, is the last act in the drama. When this substitution becomes universal, God will reveal Himself. He will arise in His majesty to shake terribly the earth. He will come out of His place to punish the inhabitants of the world for their iniquity, and the earth shall disclose her blood and shall no more cover her slain" (7T 141).

When probation closes, how complete will Satan's control of the wicked be?

"He will say to the angels, 'No longer combat Satan in his efforts to destroy. Let him work out his malignity upon the children of disobedience; for the cup of their iniquity is full' " (RH Sept. 17, 1901).

"When He leaves the sanctuary, darkness covers the inhabitants of the earth. In that fearful time the righteous must live in the sight of a holy God without an intercessor. The restraint which has been upon the wicked is removed, and Satan has entire control of the finally impenitent. God's long-suffering has ended. The world has rejected His mercy, despised His love, and trampled upon His law. The wicked have passed the boundary of their probation; the Spirit of God, persistently resisted, has been at last withdrawn. Unsheltered by divine grace, they have no protection from the wicked one" (GC 614).

How does the Bible speak of this time?

Dan. 12:1.

When the fires of passion and lawlessness escape control, what will the world be like?

"The spirit of anarchy is permeating all nations, and the outbreaks that from time to time excite the horror of the world are but indications of the pent-up fires of passion and lawlessness that, having once escaped control, will fill the earth with woe and desolation. The picture which inspiration has given of the antediluvian world represents too truly the condition to which modern society is fast hastening" (PP 102).

Is large-scale international warfare a real possibility?

Preparations for war now being made. "Everything in the world is in an unsettled state. The nations are angry, and great preparations for war are being made. Nation is plotting against nation, and kingdom against kingdom. The great day of God is hasting greatly. But although the nations are mustering their forces for war and bloodshed, the command to the angels is still in force, that they hold the four winds until the servants of God are sealed in their foreheads" (7BC 968 [1909]).

Nation will rise against nation. "Just before we entered it [the time of trouble], we all received the seal of the living God. Then I saw the four angels cease to hold the four winds. And I saw famine, pestilence and sword, nation rose against nation, and the whole world was in confusion" (*ibid.* [1846]).

Vessels will be entombed in the deep. "Four mighty angels hold back the powers of this earth till the servants of God are sealed in their foreheads. The nations of the world are eager for conflict; but they are held in check by the angels. When this restraining power is removed, there will come a time of trouble and anguish. Deadly instruments of warfare will be invented. Vessels, with their living cargo, will be entombed in the great deep. All who have not the spirit of truth will unite under the leadership of satanic agencies. But they are to be kept under control till the time shall come for the great battle of Armageddon" (*ibid.* 967).

A general engagement is coming. "Only a moment of

time, as it were, yet remains. But while already nation is rising against nation, and kingdom against kingdom, there is not now a general engagement. As yet the four winds are held until the servants of God shall be sealed in their foreheads. Then the powers of earth will marshal their forces for the last great battle" (6T 14 [see also 7BC 968]).

Is nuclear warfare a possibility?

"Satan will then plunge the inhabitants of the earth into one great, final trouble. As the angels of God cease to hold in check the fierce winds of human passion, all the elements of strife will be let loose. The whole world will be involved in ruin more terrible than that which came upon Jerusalem of old" (GC 614).

"Both the city [of Jerusalem] and the temple were razed to their foundations, and the ground upon which the holy house had stood was 'plowed like a field' (Jer. 26:18). In the siege and the slaughter that followed, more than a million of the people perished" (*ibid.* 35).

"The Saviour's prophecy concerning the visitation of judgments upon Jerusalem is to have another fulfillment, of which that terrible desolation was but a faint shadow. In the fate of the chosen city we may behold the doom of a world that has rejected God's mercy and trampled upon His law" (*ibid.* 36).

"On one occasion, when in New York City, I was in the night season called upon to behold buildings rising story after story toward heaven. These buildings were warranted to be fireproof, and they were erected to glorify their owners and builders. . . .

"The scene that next passed before me was an alarm of fire. Men looked at the lofty and supposedly fireproof buildings and said: 'They are perfectly safe.' But these buildings were consumed as if made of pitch. The fire engines could do nothing to stay the destruction. The firemen were unable to operate the engines" (9T 12, 13).

Is it possible for us to form a clear picture in our minds of the utter ruin and strife that will occur after probation closes?

"Angels are now restraining the winds of strife, that they may not blow until the world shall be warned of its coming doom; but a storm is gathering, ready to burst upon the earth; and when God shall bid His angels loose the winds, there will be such a scene of strife as no pen can picture" (Ed 179, 180 [see also 6T 408]).

Who will be blamed for all of Satan's desolating activities?

"When the angel of mercy folds her wings and departs, Satan will do the evil deeds he has long wished to do. Storm and tempest, war and bloodshed—in these things he delights, and thus he gathers in his harvest. And so completely will men be deceived by him that they will declare that these calamities are the result of the desecration of the first day of the week. From the pulpits of the popular churches will be heard the statement that the world is being punished because Sunday is not honored as it should be. And it will require no great stretch of imagination for men to believe this" (RH Sept. 17, 1901).

In addition to the havoc that God allows Satan to cause, what heaven-sent scourges will be poured out on the impenitent?

Rev. 15:1, 8; 16:1.

"I saw that the four angels would hold the four winds until Jesus' work was done in the sanctuary, and then will come the seven last plagues" (EW 36).

How dreadful will the first four plagues be?

"These plagues are not universal, or the inhabitants of the earth would be wholly cut off. Yet they will be the most awful scourges that have ever been known to mortals" (GC 628, 629).

What are the first two plagues?

Rev. 16:2, 3.

How will the wicked react to the plagues?

"The plagues were falling upon the inhabitants of the earth. Some were denouncing God and cursing Him. Others rushed to the people of God and begged to be taught how they might escape His judgments. But the saints had nothing for them. The last tear for sinners had been shed, the last agonizing prayer offered, the last burden borne, the last warning given" (EW 281).

Why will the leaders of government now determine to exterminate all commandment keepers?

"These plagues enraged the wicked against the righteous; they thought that we had brought the judgments of God upon them, and that if they could rid the earth of us, the plagues would then be stayed. A decree went forth to slay the saints, which caused them to cry day and night for deliverance. This was the time of Jacob's trouble" (*ibid.* 36, 37).

What will be God's response to the death decree?

Rev. 16:4-7.

"And 'the rivers and fountains of waters . . . became blood.' Terrible as these inflictions are, God's justice stands fully vindicated. The angel of God declares: 'Thou art righteous, O Lord, . . . because thou has judged thus. For they have shed the blood of saints and prophets, and thou hast given them blood to drink; for they are worthy (Rev. 16:4-6).' By condemning the people of God to death, they have as truly incurred the guilt of their blood as if it had been shed by their hands" (GC 628).

As the righteous flee for their lives, what is the fourth plague that God will send upon the earth?

Rev. 16:8, 9.

"In the plague that follows, power is given to the sun 'to scorch men with fire. And men were scorched with great heat (Rev. 16:8, 9).' The prophets thus describe the condition of the earth at this fearful time: '. . . The harvest of the field is perished. . . . All the trees of the field, are withered: because joy is withered away from the sons of men.' 'The seed is rotten under their clods, the garners are laid desolate. . . . How do the beasts groan! The herds of cattle are perplexed, because they have no pasture. . . . The rivers of water are dried up, and the fire hath devoured the pastures of the wilderness.' . . . 'There shall be many dead bodies in every place' (Joel 1:10-12, 7-20; Amos 8:3)" *(ibid.)*.

How will the Lord bring all the ambitions of the wicked to a sudden halt at the time of the fifth plague?

"With shouts of triumph, jeering, and imprecation, throngs of evil men are about to rush upon their prey, when, lo, a dense blackness, deeper than the darkness of the night, falls upon the earth. Then a rainbow, shining with the glory from the throne of God, spans the heavens and seems to encircle each praying company. The angry multitudes are suddenly arrested. Their mocking cries die away. The objects of their murderous rage are forgotten. With fearful forebodings they gaze upon the symbol of God's covenant and long to be shielded from its overpowering brightness" *(ibid. 635, 636)*.

Now, at the time of the sixth plague, what are the two opposing sides into which every person in the whole world has been gathered?

"Two great opposing powers are revealed in the last great battle. On one side stands the Creator of heaven and earth. All on His side bear His signet. They are obedient to His commands. On the other side stands the prince of darkness, with those who have chosen apostasy and rebellion" (7BC 982, 983).

"Evil angels unite their powers with evil men, and as they have been in constant conflict and attained an experience in the best modes of deception and battle, and have been strengthening for centuries, they will not yield the last great final contest without a desperate struggle. All the world will be on one side or the other of the question. The battle of Armageddon will be fought, and that day must find none of us sleeping. . . . The power of the Holy Ghost must be upon us, and the Captain of the Lord's host will stand at the head of the angels of heaven to direct the battle" (*ibid.* 982).

Did Satan's efforts to gather all the kings and people of the whole world under his banner begin at the time of the sixth plague, or is this the climax of long years of effort on his part?

"The enmity of Satan against good will be manifested more and more as he brings his forces into activity in his last work of rebellion; and every soul that is not fully surrendered to God, and kept by divine power, will form an alliance with Satan against heaven, and join in battle against the Ruler of the universe" (TM 465).

"The spirits of devils will go forth to the kings of the earth and to the whole world, to fasten them in deception, and urge them on to unite with Satan in his last struggle against the government of heaven" (GC 624).

"The Spirit of God is gradually withdrawing from the world. Satan is also mustering his forces of evil, going forth 'unto the kings of the earth and of the whole world,' to gather them under his banner, to be trained for 'the battle of that great day of God Almighty'" (7BC 983).

"We are to . . . understand the progress of events in the marshalling of the nations for the final conflict of the great controversy" (8T 307).

"Soon all the inhabitants of the earth will have taken sides, either for or against the government of heaven" (7T 141).

Has the God of heaven also been preparing his forces for the final battle?

"The powers of evil will not yield up the conflict without a struggle. But Providence has a part to act in the battle of Armageddon. When the earth is lighted with the glory of the angel of Revelation eighteen, the religious elements, good and evil, will awake from slumber, and the armies of the living God will take the field" (7BC 983).

Is the battle of Armageddon—the battle of that great day of God Almighty—clearly a battle between the forces of good and the forces of evil?

"A terrible conflict is before us. We are nearing the battle of the great day of God Almighty. That which has been held in control is to be let loose. The angel of mercy is folding her wings, preparing to step down from the throne, and leave the world to the control of Satan. The principalities and powers of earth are in bitter revolt against the God of heaven. They are filled with hatred against those who serve Him, and soon, very soon, will be fought the last great battle between good and evil. The earth is to be the battlefield—the scene of the final contest and the final victory. Here, where for so long Satan has led men against God, rebellion is to be forever suppressed" (RH May 13, 1902 [see also ML 308]).

Is the battle of Armageddon a real, literal battle, a "spiritual" battle, or both?

"The battles waging between the two armies are as real as those fought by the armies of this world, and on the issue of the spiritual conflict eternal destinies depend" (PK 176).

Under the seventh plague, how does the Lord take the initiative in the battle?

Rev. 16:17-21.

"The whole earth heaves and swells like the waves of the sea. Its surface is breaking up. Its very foundations seem to be giving way. Mountain chains are sinking. Inhabited islands disappear. The seaports that have become like Sodom for wickedness are swallowed up by the angry waters. . . . The proudest cities of the earth are laid low. The lordly palaces, upon which the world's great men have lavished their wealth in order to glorify themselves, are crumbling to ruin before their eyes. Prison walls are rent asunder, and God's people, who have been held in bondage for their faith, are set free.

"Graves are opened, and 'many of them that sleep in the dust of the earth . . . awake, some to everlasting life, and some to shame and everlasting contempt' (Dan. 12:2)" (GC 637).

When the followers of Satan see that everything is lost, how bitter will be their remorse?

"The rich bemoan the destruction of their grand houses. . . . No language can express the longing which the disobedient and disloyal feel for that which they have lost forever—eternal life. . . . All unite in heaping their bitterest condemnation upon the ministers. . . . The swords which were to slay God's people are now employed to destroy their enemies. Everywhere there is strife and bloodshed" (GC 654-656 [see also EW 290]).

"It is impossible to describe the horror and despair of those who have trampled upon God's holy requirements" (GC 639).

How will Christ bring all history to its grand climax?

Rev. 19:11-20.

"The battle of Armageddon is soon to be fought. He on whose vesture is written the name, King of kings and Lord of lords, leads forth the armies of heaven on white horses, clothed in fine linen, clean and white" (7BC 982).

"Soon there appears in the east a small black cloud. . . . The King of kings descends upon the clouds, wrapped in flaming fire. . . . The wicked pray to be buried beneath the rocks of the mountains. . . . The wicked are blotted from the face of the whole earth" (GC 640-657).

CHAPTER 21

HOME
AT LAST

(In this study no distinction is drawn between heaven and the new earth.)

Is heaven a real place, or is it an indefinite space, filled with intangible spirits?

Heb. 11:14, 16; 1 Peter 1:4; John 14:3.

"What a source of joy to the disciples to know that they had such a Friend in heaven to plead in their behalf! Through the visible ascension of Christ all their views and contemplation of heaven are changed. Their minds had formerly dwelt upon it as a region of unlimited space, tenanted by spirits without substance. Now heaven was connected with the thought of Jesus, whom they had loved and reverenced above all others, with whom they had conversed and journeyed, whom they had handled, even in His resurrected body. . . .

"Heaven could no longer appear to them as an indefinite, incomprehensible space, filled with intangible spirits. They now looked upon it as their future home, where mansions were being prepared for them by their loving Redeemer" (6BC 1054).

"A fear of making the future inheritance seem too material has led many to spiritualize away the very truths which lead us to look upon it as our home" (GC 674, 675).

Does Satan want us to spend time thinking about heaven?

"The temptations of Satan present earthly things and

make them all-absorbing and attractive, so that the heavenly realities are eclipsed and the attachment to the world made first" (OHC 285).

Does Christ want us to take time to think of heaven?

"Jesus comes to present the advantages and beautiful imagery of the heavenly, that the attractions of heaven shall become familiar to the thoughts, and memory's hall be hung with pictures of celestial and eternal loveliness" (*ibid.* 286).

Why has the Lord given us so much information about the future life?

"The great Teacher gives man a view of the future world. He brings it, with its attractive possessions, within the range of his vision. . . . If He can fasten the mind upon the future life and its blessedness, in comparison with the temporal concerns of this world, the striking contrast is deeply impressed upon the mind, absorbing the heart and soul and the whole being" (*ibid.* [see also OHC 250, 319]).

"Motives stronger, and agencies more powerful, could never be brought into operation; the exceeding rewards for right-doing, the enjoyment of heaven, the society of the angels, the communion and love of God and His Son, the elevation and extension of all our powers throughout eternal ages—are these not mighty incentives and encouragements to urge us to give the heart's loving service to our Creator and Redeemer?" (SC 21).

Is it possible for us to comprehend the glory of that better land?

"The wonderful things I there saw I cannot describe. Oh, that I could talk in the language of Canaan, then could

I tell a little of the glory of the better world. I saw there tables of stone in which the names of the 144,000 were engraved in letters of gold. After we beheld the glory of the temple, we went out, and Jesus left us and went to the city" (EW 19).

"Language is altogether too feeble to attempt a description of heaven. As the scene rises before me, I am lost in amazement. Carried away with the surpassing splendor and excellent glory, I lay down the pen, and exclaim, 'Oh, what love! what wondrous love!' The most exalted language fails to describe the glory of heaven or the matchless depths of a Saviour's love" (EW 289).

"If we could have but one view of the celestial city, we would never wish to dwell on earth again. There are beautiful landscapes on earth, and I enjoy all these prospects of loveliness in nature. I associate them with the Creator. But I know that if I love God, and keep His commandments, there is a far more exceeding and eternal weight of glory reserved in Heaven for me. Beautiful as are the scenes of earth, they can bear no comparison to the glories of the eternal world" (ST Apr. 8, 1889).

"Human language is inadequate to describe the reward of the righteous. It will be known only to those who behold it. No finite mind can comprehend the glory of the Paradise of God" (GC 675).

What are some of the features of nature to be found there?

Mountains, plains, and streams. "There are ever-flowing streams, clear as crystal, and beside them waving trees cast their shadows upon the paths prepared for the ransomed of the Lord. There the wide-spreading plains swell into hills of beauty, and the mountains of God rear their lofty summits. On those peaceful plains, beside those living streams, God's people, so long pilgrims and wanderers, shall find a home" *(ibid.).*

Forests. "Then we entered a wood, not like the dark woods we have here; no, no; but light, and all over glorious; the branches of the trees waved to and fro, and we all cried out, 'We will dwell safely in the wilderness and sleep in the woods.' We passed through the woods, for we were on our way to Mount Zion" (EW 18).

All kinds of trees. "Mount Zion was just before us, and on the mount was a glorious temple, and about it were seven other mountains, on which grew roses and lilies. And I saw the little ones climb, or, if they chose, use their little wings and fly, to the top of the mountains and pluck the never-fading flowers. There were all kinds of trees around the temple to beautify the place: the box, the pine, the fir, the oil, the myrtle, the pomegranate, and the fig tree bowed down with the weight of its timely figs—these made the place all over glorious" *(ibid.* 19).

All kinds of flowers. "I saw another field full of all kinds of flowers, and as I plucked them, I cried out, 'They will never fade.' Next I saw a field of tall grass, most glorious to behold; it was living green and had a reflection of silver and gold, as it waved proudly to the glory of King Jesus" *(ibid.* 18).

All kinds of fruit. "And I saw a table of pure silver; it was many miles in length, yet our eyes could extend over it. I saw the fruit of the tree of life, the manna, almonds, figs, pomegranates, grapes, and many other kinds of fruit. I asked Jesus to let me eat of the fruit" *(ibid.* 19).

The tree of life. "Here we saw the tree of life and the throne of God. Out of the throne came a pure river of water, and on either side of the river was the tree of life. On one side of the river was a trunk of a tree, and a trunk on the other side of the river, both of pure, transparent gold. At first I thought I saw two trees. I looked again, and saw that they were united at the top in one tree. So it was the tree of life on either side of the river of life. Its branches bowed to the place where we stood, and the fruit was glorious; it looked like gold mixed with silver" (*ibid.* 17).

Animals all gentle and trustful. "There shall be nothing to 'hurt nor destroy in all my holy mountain, saith the Lord (Isa. 65:25).' There man will be restored to his lost kingship, and the lower order of beings will again recognize his sway; the fierce will become gentle, and the timid trustful" (Ed 304).

Perpetual day. "The light of the sun will be superseded by a radiance which is not painfully dazzling, yet which immeasurably surpasses the brightness of our noontide. The glory of God and the Lamb floods the Holy City with unfading light. The redeemed walk in the sunless glory of perpetual day" (GC 676).

What will the people look like? How big will they be? How strong? Of what will they be capable?

About twelve feet tall. "Restored to the tree of life in the long-lost Eden, the redeemed will 'grow up' (Mal. 4:2) to the full stature of the race in its primeval glory" (*ibid.* 645).

"He [Adam] was more than twice as tall as men now living upon the earth, and was well proportioned" (3SG 34).

Twenty times as much vitality. "If Adam, at his creation, had not been endowed with twenty times as much vital force as men now have, the race, with their present habits of living in violation of natural law, would have become extinct" (FE 23).

"None will need or desire repose. There will be no weariness in doing the will of God and offering praise to His name. We shall ever feel the freshness of the morning and shall ever be far from its close" (GC 676).

"Pain cannot exist in the atmosphere of heaven. There will be no more tears, no funeral trains, no badges of mourning. 'There shall be no more death, neither sorrow, nor crying: . . . for the former things are passed away.' 'The inhabitant shall not say, I am sick' (Rev. 21:4; Isa. 33:24)" *(ibid.).*

"Heaven is all health" (3T 172).

"The acquirement of knowledge will not weary the mind or exhaust the energies" (GC 677).

Present identity perfectly preserved. "The resurrection of Jesus was a type of the final resurrection of all who sleep in Him. The countenance of the risen Saviour, His manner, His speech, were all familiar to His disciples. As Jesus arose from the dead, so those who sleep in Him are to rise again. We shall know our friends, even as the disciples knew Jesus. They may have been deformed, diseased, or disfigured, in this mortal life, and they rise in perfect health and symmetry; yet in the glorified body their identity will be perfectly preserved" (DA 804).

Perfect memories. "The antediluvians were without books, they had no written records; but with their great physical and mental vigor, they had strong memories, able to grasp and to retain that which was communicated to them, and in turn to transmit it unimpaired to their posterity" (PP 83).

Minds capable of constant expansion. "As they learn more and more of the wisdom, the love, and the power of God, their minds will be constantly expanding, and their joy will continually increase" (5T 702, 703).

Microscopic and telescopic eyesight. "With undimmed vision they gaze upon the glory of creation—suns and stars and systems, all in their appointed order circling the throne of Deity" (GC 677).

"There, when the veil that darkens our vision shall be removed, and our eyes shall behold that world of beauty of which we now catch glimpses through the microscope; when we look on the glories of the heavens, now scanned afar through the telescope; when, the blight of sin removed, the whole earth shall appear in 'the beauty of the Lord our God,' what a field will be open to our study!" (Ed 303).

"The veil that interposes between the visible and the invisible world will be drawn aside, and wonderful things will be revealed" (*ibid.* 304).

Ability to travel through space. "The redeemed throng will range from world to world, and much of their time will be employed in searching out the mysteries of redemption" (7BC 990).

"All the treasures of the universe will be open to the study of God's redeemed. Unfettered by mortality, they wing their tireless flight to worlds afar" (GC 677).

A crown of life. "The reward, the glories of heaven, bestowed upon the overcomers, will be proportionate to the degree in which they have represented the character of Christ to the world. 'He which soweth sparingly shall reap also sparingly' (2 Cor. 9:6). . . . The crown of life will be bright or dim, will glitter with many stars, or be lighted by few gems, in accordance with our own course of action" (OHC 123).

Will there be family life, marriages, and births?

Matt. 22:23-30.

No marriages or births. "There are men today who express their belief that there will be marriages and births in the new earth, but those who believe the Scriptures cannot accept such doctrine. The doctrine that children will be born in the new earth is not a part of the 'sure word of prophecy'" (MM 99 [1SM 172]).

Not to speculate where we have no information.

"Workers for God should not spend time speculating as to what conditions will prevail in the new earth. It is presumption to indulge in suppositions and theories regarding matters that the Lord has not revealed. He has made every provision for our happiness in the future life, and we are not to speculate regarding His plans for us. Neither are we to measure the conditions of the future life by the conditions of this life" (GW 314).

"It is presumption to indulge in suppositions and theories regarding matters that God has not made known to us in His Word. We need not enter into speculation regarding our future state" (1SM 173).

Little children taken to heaven. "As the little infants come forth immortal from their dusty beds, they immediately wing their way to their mother's arms. They meet again nevermore to part. But many of the little ones have no mother there. We listen in vain for the rapturous song of triumph from the mother. The angels receive the motherless infants and conduct them to the tree of life" (2SM 260).

Little children in the new earth. "And I saw the little ones climb, or, if they chose, use their little wings and fly, to the top of the mountains and pluck the never-fading flowers" (EW 19).

Reunited with our friends. "Friends long separated by death are united, nevermore to part, and with songs of gladness ascend together to the city of God" (GC 645).

Will live in houses. "Then we began to look at the glorious things outside of the city. There I saw most glorious houses, that had the appearance of silver, supported by four pillars set with pearls most glorious to behold. These were to be inhabited by the saints. In each was a golden shelf. I saw many of the saints go into the houses, take off their glittering crowns and lay them on the shelf" (EW 18).

197

" 'They shall build houses and inhabit them' (Isa. 65:21)" (GC 675).

With whom will we enjoy face-to-face communion?

Our guardian angel. "Every redeemed one will understand the ministry of angels in his own life. The angel who was his guardian from his earliest moment; the angel who watched his steps, and covered his head in the day of peril; the angel who was with him in the valley of the shadow of death, who marked his resting place, who was the first to greet him in the resurrection morning—what will it be to hold converse with him, and to learn the history of divine interposition in the individual life, of heavenly cooperation in every work for humanity!" (Ed 305).

"From what dangers, seen and unseen, we have been preserved through the interposition of the angels, we shall never know, until in the light of eternity we see the providences of God" (DA 240).

The other angels and the faithful of all ages. "The loves and sympathies which God Himself has planted in the soul shall there find truest and sweetest exercise. The pure communion with holy beings, the harmonious social life with the blessed angels and with the faithful ones of all ages who have washed their robes and made them white in the blood of the Lamb, the sacred ties that bind together 'the whole family in heaven and earth' (Eph. 3:15)—these help to constitute the happiness of the redeemed" (GC 677 [see also Ed 306]).

The Father and the Son. "The people of God are privileged to hold open communion with the Father and the Son. . . . We shall see Him face to face, without a dimming veil between" (GC 676, 677).

"If, during this life, they are loyal to God, they will at last 'see his face; and his name shall be in their foreheads'

(Rev. 22:4). And what is the happiness of heaven but to see God? What greater joy could come to the sinner saved by the grace of Christ than to look upon the face of God and know Him as Father?" (8T 268).

What one reminder of the cruel work of sin will ever be before us?

"One reminder alone remains: Our Redeemer will ever bear the marks of His crucifixion. Upon His wounded head, upon His side, His hands and feet, are the only traces of the cruel work that sin has wrought" (GC 674).

"Though the griefs and pains and temptations of earth are ended and the cause removed, the people of God will ever have a distinct, intelligent knowledge of what their salvation has cost" (*ibid.* 651).

What activities and studies will we engage in?

Gather regularly to worship God. " 'And it shall come to pass, that from one new moon to another, and from one sabbath to another, shall all flesh come to worship before me, saith the Lord' (Isa. 66:23)" (PK 733).

Create and hear the most perfect music. "Then I saw a very great number of angels bring from the city glorious crowns—a crown for every saint, with his name written thereon. As Jesus called for the crowns, angels presented them to Him, and with His own right hand, the lovely Jesus placed the crowns on the heads of the saints. In the same manner the angels brought the harps, and Jesus presented them also to the saints. The commanding angels first struck the note, and then every voice was raised in grateful, happy praise, and every hand skillfully swept over the strings of the harp, sending forth melodious music in rich and perfect strains" (EW 288).

"There will be music there, and song, such music and song as, save in the visions of God, no mortal ear has heard or mind conceived" (Ed 307 [see also PK 730]).

Study the history of the great controversy. "Then will be opened before him the course of the great conflict that had its birth before time began, and that ends only when time shall cease" (Ed 304).

Discover the reason for all this life's perplexities. "All the perplexities of life's experience will then be made plain. Where to us have appeared only confusion and disappointment, broken purposes and thwarted plans, will be seen a grand, overruling, victorious purpose, a divine harmony" (*ibid.* 305).

Learn the outworking of every good deed in this life. "There all who have wrought with unselfish spirit will behold the fruit of their labors. The outworking of every right principle and noble deed will be seen. Something of this we see here. But how little of the result of the world's noblest work is in this life manifest to the doer! How many toil unselfishly and unweariedly for those who pass beyond their reach and knowledge! Parents and teachers lie down in their last sleep, their lifework seeming to have been wrought in vain; they know not that their faithfulness has unsealed springs of blessing that can never cease to flow; only by faith they see the children they have trained become a benediction and an inspiration to their fellow men, and the influence repeat itself a thousandfold.

"Many a worker sends out into the world messages of strength and hope and courage, words that carry blessing to hearts in every land; but of the results he, toiling in loneliness and obscurity, knows little. So gifts are bestowed, burdens are borne, labor is done. Men sow the seed from which, above their graves, others reap blessed harvests. They plant trees, that others may eat the fruit. They are content here to know that they have set in motion agencies for good. In the hereafter the action and reaction of all these will be seen" (*ibid.* 305, 306).

Work in garden and field. "In the earth made new, the redeemed will engage in the occupations and pleasures that brought happiness to Adam and Eve in the beginning. The Eden life will be lived, the life in garden and field" (PK 730, 731 [see also Ed 304]).

"I saw many of the saints go into the houses, take off their glittering crowns and lay them on the shelf, then go out into the field by the houses to do something with the earth; not as we have to do with the earth here; no, no. A glorious light shone all about their heads, and they were continually shouting and offering praises to God" (EW 18).

Study all the treasures of the universe. "All the treasures of the universe will be open to the study of God's children. With unutterable delight we shall enter into the joy and the wisdom of unfallen beings. We shall share the treasures gained through ages upon ages spent in contemplation of God's handiwork. And the years of eternity, as they roll, will continue to bring more glorious revelations" (Ed 307 [see also GC 677, 678]).

Constantly develop with no end ever in sight. "There every power will be developed, every capability increased. The grandest enterprises will be carried forward, the loftiest aspirations will be reached, the highest ambitions realized. And still there will arise new heights to surmount, new wonders to admire, new truths to comprehend, fresh objects to call forth the powers of body and mind and soul" (Ed 307 [see also GC 677]).

What will be the chief joy of the redeemed?

"Everything in heaven is noble and elevated. All seek

the interest and happiness of others. No one devotes himself to looking out and caring for self. It is the chief joy of all holy beings to witness the joy and happiness of those around them" (2T 239).

How can I be sure to be there?

"It should be the determination of every soul, not so much to seek to understand all about the conditions that will prevail in the future state, as to know what the Lord requires of him in this life" (CT 249).

"The peace and harmony of the heavenly courts will not be marred by the presence of one who is rough or unkind. He who in this world exalts self in the work given him to do will never see the kingdom of God unless he is changed in spirit, unless he becomes meek and lowly, revealing the simplicity of a little child" (8T 140).

"If you are to be saints in heaven, you must first be saints upon the earth" (TM 145).